Although we will not get
time, we must never stop
best place to learn is at the

'A great quote from this very practical book
target in helping readers to grow in their faith. Whether they
are at the start of their "new life" or want an injection of
encouragement, this straightforward book gives the material
that is needed. It's clear and accessible to all, and I can see it
being helpful in many situations. The questions, application
and prayer at the end of each chapter are great practical
material and easy to use for one-to-one or small-group
discussions.

'As a youth fellowship leader and elder, this is a book I
would be glad to use in all sorts of situations.'
*Trevor Long OBE, Clerk of Session at Rosemary Presbyterian Church,
and Clerk of the North Belfast Presbytery*

'Carolyn Dawson leads us on a gentle exploration of Christ's
teaching, helping us to marvel afresh at the Son of God, and
encouraging us to consider where there may be room for
improvement in our own lives. Carolyn's approach is simple:
let's listen to Jesus' words and practise them. A great book
for those young in the faith and those older!'
David Wilson, National Director at Precept Ireland

'Our generation values customisation, personal shoppers,
individual playlists and on-demand TV, all from a broad
spectrum of choice. The concept of a "narrow path" is
counterintuitive and immediately unattractive in this context.
However (as Carolyn articulates so well), it is this narrow
path alone that offers life. In the pages of this book, you will
be encouraged to connect with the Scriptures, encounter
Jesus and consider how to follow Him in practical ways. Life
in all its fullness is only available in Jesus.

'Carolyn shows how following Him (to the exclusion of all others) is the only path to redemption, reconciliation and eternal union with God. Jesus said that only a few find this narrow path.

'This book is a gift to the Church, and I trust it will serve as a signpost away from the broad road, away from destruction and to the small gate and the narrow path where Life is found.'

Michael Wylie, Pastor, Greenisland Baptist Church

'In the Christian faith, we need to know who we are following, and this book helps to unpack the key truths about who Jesus is, to emphasise his major claims and to encourage us towards the basic means by which his followers will grow.

'Carolyn writes with clarity and has brought us a book saturated with Scripture, timeless in truth and accessible to all, regardless of age, stage or background. *The Narrow Path* will be a helpful tool for those who seek to grow in their own journey of discipleship. The questions at the end of each chapter offer opportunities for further personal reflection or group discussion. I heartily commend it to you.'

Rick Hill, Presbyterian Church in Ireland (Council for Mission in Ireland); author of Deep Roots of Resilient Disciples

The Narrow Path

Carolyn Dawson

instant
ap[]stle

First published in Great Britain in 2024

Instant Apostle
104A The Drive
Rickmansworth
Herts
WD3 4DU

British Library Cataloguing-in-Publication Data

A catalogue record for this book is available from the British Library.

This book and all other Instant Apostle books are available from Instant Apostle:

Website: www.instantapostle.com

Email: info@instantapostle.com

ISBN 978-1-912726-85-1

Printed in Great Britain.

*I will instruct you and teach you
in the way you should go;
I will counsel you with my eye
upon you.*

(Psalm 32:8)

Contents

Foreword

When I played rugby at school, we had a coach who would always say the same thing when we got overconfident, made things too complicated or messed up, and it was this:

Go back to basics!

There can come a point in life when things can feel overwhelming or too complicated, or we go through a period of it feeling like it's (or we have) messed up!

This book is a call to go back to basics. Whether you're exploring Christian faith and feel that life is overwhelming and you want answers, whether you've been a Christian for a long time and all of a sudden it seems very complicated or whether you're a new Christian and it can seem like all you do is mess up as you try to figure out what it's all about.

When Carolyn came to me to say she was writing this, she came with the same humility, teachability and earnestness that you'll see flow from the pages of this book. As the book has developed, so has she. Everything she is talking about is something she wants to see in her own life, and in a world where integrity is in short supply, this is something admirable to witness! In everything written, she wants to point you to Jesus: His purpose, His vision, His teaching, His impact, His way.

You'll see this and lots more, including the reason we need the teacher in the first place.

To go back to basics means hearing clearly what Jesus shares in what it means to follow Him. There's no sugar coating it; some parts you read will be hard hitting (as you think about the cost and commitment), some parts will be challenging (as you consider your own attitude), some parts will be practical and encouraging (prayer and service) and others will provide vision (as you think about God's kingdom).

Why not pick it up and read, not just for yourself but perhaps there is someone you could read this with. There are helpful reflective questions at the end of each chapter as well as practical applications and prayers to guide you through.

And so, as the title says, the path is narrow, but I hope and pray that you will also find through the pages of this book that the foundation is deep and, praise God, that the teacher can be trusted!

Phil Howe, Discipleship Pastor, Greenisland Baptist Church

Introduction

Do you remember what you were doing when you were eleven or twelve years old? The transition period between primary and secondary school when everything was both a little scary and exciting at the same time. You were in 'big school' now, and yet 'big' was not how you felt because, once again, you were back to being among the youngest members of the school. Confidence can often take a bit of a knock and it can take some time to get that back in place.

In Luke 2, we come across a boy of a similar age, who apparently was not lacking in confidence at all. His name was Jesus, and He was sitting in the temple at Jerusalem listening to the teachers, as well as asking and answering questions. Luke tells us that, 'all who heard him were amazed at his understanding and his answers' (Luke 2:47). Eighteen years later He would reveal who He truly was as He travelled across the whole region teaching in the synagogues and proclaiming the gospel of the kingdom of God. He went from listening to teachers to being the teacher. Unfortunately, not everyone would realise that they were being taught by the Son of God and that His teachings would lead them back to the Father.

Yet there were many who, as soon as they heard Jesus, would follow Him to the next town or village to hear Him again, such was their hunger for teaching and for leadership. Just like today, the people at that time were not short of teachers or rabbis. There may have been synagogues in every town, and religious leaders aplenty, but it was still as if they were 'in a dry and weary land where there is no water' (Psalm

63:1). The people had an unquenched thirst and something within told them that Jesus was the well at which they should drink.

> Blessed are those who hunger and thirst for righteous,
> for they shall be satisfied.
> (Matthew 5:6)

Does your soul thirst for the Lord? Do you have a deep hunger to know and understand His Word? Sitting at the feet of Jesus is an incredible experience, for He is the greatest teacher you will ever have. Whether you are a new Christian or simply exploring the fundamentals of your faith, let Jesus teach you what it means to be a disciple, and let the truth of His words seep into your soul. If your faith needs a boost, He can fill you with boldness and strength, or if you just feel a bit lost, He can get you back on track.

The lessons of Jesus are forthright, challenging and often tough, but what they produce is a deep-rooted life of faith which stands on a solid foundation. Christ is our cornerstone,[1] and every lesson that He gives helps us to build a strong and steadfast faith. The Christian life is not an easy one; there are days of joy and days of sorrow; there are great achievements and great failures; there is love and there is hurt. We all have amazing times when life is lived on the mountaintop, and we also have the reality of days that are lived in the shadow of the valley.[2] Our journeys will all be different but, as children of God, our destination is the same.

I hope that through the pages of this book and in the company of those first twelve disciples, your understanding of the gospel truth will grow deeper as you get to know Jesus better. There are so many wonderful verses to help guide our daily lives as followers of Christ, and of those I have barely

---

[1] Ephesians 2:20; 1 Peter 2:6-7.
[2] See Psalm 23:4.

scratched the surface. God's Word brings us valuable lessons which instruct us in the outward expressions of love, compassion, forgiveness and respect towards others, as well as inward expressions of repentance and faithfulness towards God. Through all of these, we spread the beautiful fragrance of Christ wherever we go; a fragrance that is pleasing to God.[3] The Lord Jesus walked in a manner worthy of His calling and fully pleasing to the Father. He is our example in every aspect of life, from first step to last breath. When Jesus gave Himself as the offering on the altar of Calvary, it was 'a fragrant offering and sacrifice to God' (Ephesians 5:2). When we follow His example and offer our whole lives to God, we too become a pleasing aroma to the Father, for we carry the fragrance of Jesus within us.

Although we will not get everything right all of the time, we must never stop pursuing that goal, and the best place to learn is at the feet of Jesus. Having experienced the realities of this earthly life, He understands the pressures and conflicts, the hurts and the joys, the relationships and all of the daily interactions that we will have. The best thing we can do for ourselves is to let Him teach us as He opens up the truth of His Word and then to let that truth fill our hearts and minds.

What a privilege it was for those first disciples, listening firsthand to the teachings of Jesus, some of whom exclaimed, 'Did not our hearts burn within us while he talked to us on the road, while he opened to us the Scriptures?' (Luke 24:32). Just imagine listening to the Word of God being recited by the Son of God; the power of it causing your heart to burn. God's Word truly is kindling for the soul. When we read the Bible, believing it to be the spoken Word of God and allowing it to penetrate our innermost being, it still has the ability to set our hearts on fire.

---

[3] 2 Corinthians 2:14-15.

My prayer for you is that as the Lord leads you forward in faith, His beautiful fragrance will spill out from you to the world around and onto everyone you meet.

Every blessing for the journey.
Carolyn

1
Why the Teacher was needed

For this purpose I was born and for this purpose I have come into the world – to bear witness to the truth.
(John 18:37)

Throughout this book, we will essentially be looking at the 'who, what, where, why and when' in relation to Jesus, and the 'how' in relation to ourselves. In these first few chapters we are going to consider some of the reasons why it was necessary for Him to come to us personally, who He is specifically, and what it means to put our faith in Him completely. As Christians, unless we understand the fundamental elements of our faith, we will be unable to have that faith worked out in a practical and meaningful way. So let's jump right in and discover why Jesus came.

In the Old Testament, we encounter a God who spoke to people on a one-to-one basis. Adam, Cain, Enoch, Noah, Abraham, Hagar, Moses, Joshua... and the list goes on. As time moved on and the people strayed further from God, He appointed judges and kings, prophets and priests to carry His words to the people and to lead them on the right path. Fast-forward to the New Testament and we find that the scribes and Pharisees are the ones who should be leading by example, teaching the truth of the Scriptures and steering the people in the way they should go.

Unfortunately, these leaders did not practise what they preached, which meant that their teaching was more in the way of, 'Do as I say, not as I do.' The people were following 'blind guides' (Matthew 15:14) who were leading them deeper into darkness and away from the light of truth. God did not want His people being led further astray through the teaching of hypocrites, and being well aware of the darkness that would envelop them, He had put a plan in place for the light to be sent.

Back in the eighth century BC, God spoke through His prophet Isaiah, saying:

> Arise, shine, for your light has come,
> and the glory of the LORD has risen upon you.
> For behold, darkness shall cover the earth,
> and thick darkness the peoples;
> but the LORD will arise upon you,
> and his glory will be seen upon you.
> (Isaiah 60:1-2)

Jesus was the promised light who came to fulfil the truth of the prophecies, proclaim the truth of the Father, explain the truth of the kingdom and declare the truth of the gospel. He came from His place in the heavens to walk among the people on earth, to be God's glorious light, so that we would no longer stumble around in the dark. He came to open our ears to the truth of the Scriptures so that no one would be led astray, and to open our hearts to the love and compassion of the Father, so that we would not remain a broken people.

Jesus came to remove the scales from our eyes, lift the burdens from our shoulders, quench the thirst of our souls and set us free from the bondage of sin. He came to redeem us and lead us back to the Father.

Removing the scales

*Do not marvel that I said to you, 'You must be born
again.'*
(John 3:7)

As we read through the Gospels, it becomes evident that a
large proportion of the time that Jesus spent teaching was to
the masses. However, belief is a personal decision and it leads
Jesus to some fascinating encounters and one-on-one
conversations. In John 3 we are given access to one of those
personal interactions that leads to one of the most well-
known verses in the whole Bible – John 3:16. The
conversation we get to listen in on takes place between Jesus
and a Pharisee called Nicodemus.

Throughout the Gospels we see the disappointment that
Jesus feels towards the Pharisees, and His description of
them is often less than flattering. Like any group, though,
there are always those within it that think slightly differently
or who are open to the possibilities of 'what if'. Nicodemus
was one of those men. He knew the Scriptures and he had
watched and listened to this rabbi and… well… there was
something, but could it truly be…?

It's possible Nicodemus had spoken to other colleagues
who had dismissed his thoughts as ludicrous, but others were
having the same feeling. They needed to know who this
intriguing rabbi truly was, so Nicodemus agreed to go (or
possibly drew the short straw) to speak to Jesus privately. It
was decided that under the cover of night would probably be
less conspicuous.

When Jesus and he met, he acknowledged that there were
those among the Pharisees who had come to believe that
Jesus was indeed 'a teacher come from God' (John 3:2).
Although this was a step in the right direction, their eyes had
not yet been fully opened because, as yet, they had not been
born of the Spirit. Jesus explained this to him, saying, 'unless

one is born again he cannot see the kingdom of God' (John 3:3). First you are born in flesh (natural human birth), then you must be born in Spirit (supernatural spiritual birth). Nicodemus was bewildered and may have felt that for all his studying, he knew very little. Jesus then presented the truth in its most simple form:

> For God so loved the world, that he gave his only Son, that whoever believes in him should not perish but have eternal life.
> (John 3:16)

Nicodemus had a lot to work through because everything that he thought he knew needed a rethink. He came to Jesus in the darkness (literally and figuratively), but he left enlightened because he had come to the true light; he just didn't fully realise it yet. The great thing about this conversation is that this personal encounter with Jesus appears to have ignited something within Nicodemus to continue searching for the truth. [4] The final time we encounter Nicodemus he is with Joseph of Arimathea and they are taking the body of Jesus to wrap it in linen cloths with spices and then place Him in a new tomb.[5] Would he do this if the scales had not fallen from his eyes to reveal who Jesus really was?

We should never get hung up on what we think we know, and we should avoid getting carried along with the crowd. There is always something more to learn and something new to discover, so never lose the fire within to search further and dig deeper.

Studying the Bible, especially if we are a new Christian, can seem like a daunting task, and it can sometimes feel as if we are reading a manual of dos and don'ts. This can often be overwhelming, so having people around who can help steer

---

[4] John 7:50-51.
[5] John 19:38-42.

us in the right direction is essential, because regardless of whether we are young or old in the faith, we all need spiritual guidance.

The Lord calls and equips leaders to guide His flock. It is a true blessing to be in a fellowship with a great teacher of the Scriptures who helps us understand the Word of God and really brings it to life. Someone who not only tells us what the Bible says, but is also able to show us what that looks like in our day-to-day lives. Church leaders have the same commission that was given to the disciple Peter, to feed and look after us, the lambs and the sheep.[6] (We will look further at the analogy of shepherd and sheep in Chapter Two.)

Pastoral leaders study the Word of God, glean its insights, promises, instructions and truths, and then they bring these truths from God's heart to ours. Christian maturity develops as these seeds of truth grow, and growth continues through a deeper understanding of God and His Word. Seek out great teachers of Scripture, and each time the seeds of God's truth are sown into your life, ask the Lord to cultivate them so that the roots become stronger and your understanding grows deeper.

Lifting the burden

Come to me, all who labour and are heavy laden, and
I will give you rest.
(Matthew 11:28)

Our bodies all need a certain amount of rest; while we sleep, for example, the body has time to repair itself, rebuild energy stores and restore its optimum working levels. During the time of Jesus' ministry, the majority of those listening would have had very physical jobs: fishermen, carpenters, stonemasons, field workers, etc. They were accustomed to a

---

[6] John 21:15-17.

hard day's labour and would have understood the need for rest. Jesus always used everyday situations to help people visualise His teaching, and He spoke right into the heart of their concerns.

Addressing the leaders of the people, Jesus said to them, 'You load people with burdens hard to bear, and you yourselves do not touch the burdens with one of your fingers' (Luke 11:46). These spiritual leaders were a law unto themselves and, as previously noted, their motto appeared to be, 'Do as I say, not as I do.' They made the law a burden, and there were so many things to get wrong that the people couldn't keep up with all the rules. This angered Jesus, who likened them to 'unmarked graves' (Luke 11:44), because how is anyone supposed to know they are walking in the wrong place if it is not clearly marked?

In contrast to Jesus, these other leaders appeared to make life as difficult as they could for the people. Jesus could see their struggle, and so, with tenderness and compassion, He looked at each one and said:

> Come to me ... and I will give you rest. Take my yoke upon you, and learn from me, for I am gentle and lowly in heart, and you will find rest for your souls. For my yoke is easy, and my burden is light.
> (Matthew 11:28-30)

'Learn from me.' There is no better teacher to have than Christ Himself; a pure example of gentleness and humility. As we follow Jesus through the Gospels, ministering and interacting with those deemed to be unworthy, and as we watch how He treats the outcast, the sick, the poor and the sinful, we get a beautiful picture of what it means to be gentle and lowly in heart. Jesus was given all power and authority, and yet He 'made himself nothing, taking the form of a servant' (Philippians 2:7). This is strength manifested through a humble nature, and Jesus wants us to rest in that strength. What He offers is not just physical rest, for when we come to Him, we receive rest for the soul.

Life gets so busy; it can often become chaotic and everything around us can just feel like noise. We try to do things in our own strength, which is exhausting, and then we wonder why we are constantly tired. Each one of us needs rest for our bodies, rest for our minds and rest for our souls. Without rest we burn out, become unproductive or ineffective and we are unable to function properly. Resting in Jesus not only refreshes us physically and mentally, it also strengthens us spiritually. When we are yoked to His Word and learn from Him, we are brought into a divine sanctuary of deep inner rest.

Quenching the thirst

Jesus stood up and cried out, 'If anyone thirsts, let him come to me and drink.'
(John 7:37)

Hunger and thirst are things that people can instantly relate to. During His ministry, Jesus travelled extensively and, like all other travellers, He would have known where the wells were situated throughout the region, so as to refill the waterbags. One such well (known as Jacob's well) was situated just outside Sychar, in Samaria. It was at this well that Jesus spoke with a Samaritan woman about living water that would take away all thirst – but it was water that did not come from Jacob's well. The woman had noticed that the man speaking to her did not appear to have a vessel to draw with, prompting her to ask where this water was coming from. In reply, Jesus told her that the water comes from Him and is 'a spring of water welling up to eternal life' (John 4:14).

A little further on in John's Gospel we hear Jesus continue the theme of living water, during the Feast of Booths at Jerusalem. (The Feast of Booths was a time of remembering the forty years in the wilderness, a time of thanksgiving for God's provision and a time of prayer for the rains for the next year's harvest.) Jesus wanted all those who were listening to recognise the drought in their own lives and their need for life-giving water. You can sense the urgency in His voice as He stands and cries out, 'If anyone thirsts, let him come to me and drink' (John 7:37). Rabbis would normally sit and teach, so this immediately feels different as Jesus continues earnestly calling to the people, saying, 'Whoever believes in me, as the Scripture has said, "Out of his heart will flow rivers of living water"' (John 7:38).

There were those among the crowd who responded and believed that Jesus really was the Christ, and I wonder if they, perhaps, recalled the words of the prophet Zechariah or Isaiah, who declared:

> On that day there shall be a fountain opened for the house of David and the inhabitants of Jerusalem, to cleanse them from sin and uncleanness.
> (Zechariah 13:1)

> With joy you will draw water from the wells of salvation. And you will say in that day:
> 'Give thanks to the LORD.'
> (Isaiah 12:3)

This invitation from Jesus is continually offered and the fountain of life is available to all who thirst for truth, who seek forgiveness and who long to be filled with the ever-flowing streams of living water that come from the Spirit of God. Those who accept the invitation become the vessel into which the water wells up and runs over, immersing them in God's abundant life. Blessed indeed is everyone who has a hunger for God's Word and a thirst for His righteousness, 'for they shall be satisfied' (Matthew 5:6).

The thirst for satisfaction

The need to find satisfaction is something that we all experience in different areas of our life. Mick Jagger couldn't find any, but I don't think he was looking in the right places! For everyone looking to be satisfied, there is a company or an organisation trying to fill that need. Once we try their product or service, they will often ask for a customer satisfaction survey to be completed. This will have a list of topics and an area of service within each one, from which we choose whether we have been: highly satisfied; satisfied; neither satisfied nor dissatisfied; dissatisfied; highly dissatisfied.

The questions in the survey could be for the helpfulness of staff or the cleanliness of a room, the wait time for an order or the overall level of service, etc. The problem with some surveys is the length of them, and halfway through we end up just ticking the middle option randomly in order to get it finished. The truth is, we mostly vote with our feet. When we find a shop, restaurant or hotel that ticks the right boxes, a place that satisfies our needs, we will keep going back.

We have so many different kinds of needs on a purely physical level. We need food, water, rest, company, activity, sleep, security, belonging, warmth, love, friendship and much more. If you had to fill in a survey for this list, how would it look? Are you highly satisfied in each of these areas? On top of the physical we also have deep spiritual needs that require attention, although sometimes we don't even recognise that the thing we long for is in fact spiritual satisfaction.

When we come to God, it is often our wants that we bring to His attention first: 'I want to see this particular thing happen, I want to go to this particular place, I want to do this particular thing...' which may all be good, but through continual reading of God's Word we begin to recognise our true needs, and all those 'wants' condense down to just one: 'Lord, I want to live according to Your ways.' 'Blessed are you,' says the Lord, 'for in this you will truly be satisfied.' Philippians 4:19 says, 'God will supply every need of yours according to his riches in glory in Christ Jesus', and what Jesus is saying in Matthew 5:6 is that He will supply every spiritual thirst that we have, according to the eternal riches of God.

One of my favourite movie quotes emphasises the point that people are looking for genuine leaders, but if those leaders can't be found they'll listen to whoever steps up to speak. This search for leadership is like a deep thirst, and when it can't be quenched, people are willing to drink the sand because, ultimately, they can't tell the difference.[7]

Jesus travelled through a 'dry and weary land' (Psalm 63:1) in which the people were, in effect, drinking the sand. This is still true in society today. People crave leadership and direction; they thirst for someone or something to follow, and in the absence of real leadership they will listen to anyone who steps forward with the offer of fulfilment. Jesus is the only one who can fulfil our needs, the only one who can quench our thirst and the only one who can satisfy the deep longings of our soul. Looking for satisfaction anywhere other than through Jesus will ultimately result in disappointment. He alone is the pure source of abundant life; a well we can drink from that never runs dry.

Setting us free

So if the Son sets you free, you will be free indeed.
(John 8:36)

Jesus would often be found speaking in the temple from early morning; knowing this, the Pharisees came on one particular morning to purposely disrupt His teaching. With callous

---

[7] *The American President* (1995). Directed by Rob Reiner, distributed by Columbia Pictures.

disregard to the woman in their grip, they dragged her to the temple, amplifying her humiliation, and dropped her at the feet of Jesus. In exposing her shame of adultery to everyone present, their not-so-subtle approach was just another test by the religious leaders to discredit Jesus. Unfortunately for them, all they managed to do was expose their own ignorance and arrogance. The accusers left defeated in their cause, and the woman was set free from condemnation.[8] We don't know what happened next in this woman's life, but if she heeded the Lord's instruction and turned completely from her sin, she would have experienced true freedom.

As Jesus continued to teach, He spoke to the people about the darkness of their sin and the fact that they were lost in it. He longed for them to realise the gravity of their situation and that their future depended on their response. No one needed to remain lost because the light was before them, leading them out of the dark. John 8:30 tells us, 'As he was saying these things, many believed in him.' Jesus knew that, with some, this belief was tenuous at best, so He said to them:

> If you abide in my word, you are truly my disciples, and you will know the truth, and the truth will set you free.
> (John 8:31-32)

This confused the people because, as far as they were concerned, they had never been enslaved to anyone. For them, it would have made no sense for Jesus to say they would be set free. Set free from what exactly? Jesus pointed out their slavery to sin and invited them to visualise a house with a master, a son and a slave. They knew the definition of a slave – one who is completely subject to another, without the means of freeing oneself. Within the master's house, a son would have all the privileges and freedom while the slave

---

[8] John 8:2-11.

would have none. The son would receive the inheritance while the slave would only inherit a new master.

Just as Jesus wanted to free the people back then, He still wants to free people here and now. He offers freedom from unseen chains and the privilege of being changed from slaves to sons and daughters of God. The inheritance of God's kingdom was and is available to all who accept Jesus at His word and believe the truth of His gospel. Knowing the truth and being set free is a promise to every one of us when we follow Him, remain in Him and stay within His teaching.

God's Word does not merely illuminate truth, it *is* truth, and that truth brings a freedom that most of us have not fully embraced. This concept of living free is hard for people to understand because, just like the Jewish people in John 8, most do not see themselves as being enslaved to anyone or anything. In his opening sentence of *The Social Contract*, the philosopher Jean-Jacques Rousseau said, 'Man is born free but everywhere he is in chains.'[9] Rousseau may have been ahead of the curve in seeing the slavery of mankind, but he misunderstood his freedom. In contrast, the truth that Jesus was explaining was that we were not born free but born captive, and 'everyone who commits sin is a slave to sin' (John 8:34). From the very beginning with Adam and Eve in the garden of Eden, and continuing today, the devil twists God's truth to cause doubt in our minds. As soon as we think that we have nothing to be freed from, the deception grows.

The devil delights in deceiving the Christian most of all. When we become aware of our sin, the devil switches tactics so that we don't forget about it. He moves from the deception regarding sin to the deception regarding forgiveness. He manages to keep past sin in our thoughts in order to encourage continued guilt, and he plays on our self-

---

[9] Jean-Jacques Rousseau, *Du contrat social; ou, Principes du droit politique* (1762). See also *The Social Contract*, Book 1, Chapter 1, www.sparknotes.com/philosophy/socialcontract/full-text/book-i-chapter-i (accessed 4th July 2024)

doubts. He tells us we are not good enough. He whispers at the prayer meeting, 'Don't pray out loud, you'll only make a fool of yourself.' When we sit in study group we hear that niggling voice say, 'Just stay quiet, you're not at the same level as everyone else.' It is so easy for the devil to be convincing because we so often feel the weight of our own inadequacies, but it is all lies.

Just like the woman who was caught in her sin and who, after her accusers left, was set free from condemnation, we too can experience true freedom. Freedom from lies, freedom from accusations, freedom from guilt and freedom from slavery. Slavery? Yes, slavery.

We are slaves to anything that has a hold on our life, be it gambling, alcohol, drugs, along with other things that we might laugh off or dismiss, like food, shopping, laziness, jealousy and gossiping. There are so many things that the devil uses to enslave us, and from which Jesus longs to set us free. Do not hold on to the things for which Jesus spilled His blood. His death bought our freedom. He bowed to the will of the Father, enduring scorn, humiliation, mutilation and anguish, and then He went down to the depths of Death and Hades so that we might be released from its grasp.[10] He did absolutely everything that was required of Him to ensure our freedom. Then, having felt abandoned under the weight and darkness of our sin, He emerged victorious and was lifted to the place of supremacy, at the right hand of the Father.

Why was the teacher needed? He was needed then for the same reasons that He is needed today. Scales still need to be removed from blind eyes; burdens still need to be lifted from weary shoulders; the thirst of the soul still needs to be quenched and the slave of sin still needs to be set free. So don't let the 'father of lies' (John 8:44) blind you, burden you, rob you or deceive you. Make a habit of reading God's Word on a continual basis and let the truth of it set you free.

---

[10] Revelation 1:18; see also 1 Peter 3:18-19.

Reflections

Questions

- Think back to a time when you thought about something differently from those around you. Did you have the confidence to express your opinion, or did you allow yourself to get carried along with the crowd? Did that changed things for you going forward?

- When it comes to stepping out of the busyness of life, what kind of 'restful' activity do you find beneficial, and how often do Jesus and/or spiritual things play a part in any of that?

- What kinds of burdens are you still carrying that you wish you could simply hand over to Jesus?

Practical application

Note down any areas of your life in which you feel the enemy is still holding you captive. Consider what it is you need in order to move forward in the freedom that Jesus offers and then ask God to help you in each of the areas you have written down. Keep a note of your progress. It could also help to speak to a trusted leader about these things.

Prayer

Lord, I want to understand all that Your Word teaches. Please help me to see Your truth clearly and to never be afraid to speak it out. Help me to hand over all the things that weigh on my mind and which stop me resting fully in You. Show me how to live in Your freedom and give me a continual thirst to know You more. Amen.

2
The Teacher's credentials

*When you have lifted up the Son of Man, then you will
know that I am he, and that I do nothing on my own
authority, but speak just as the Father taught me.*
(John 8:28)

We now know why Jesus came, but who exactly is this great
orator, and under what authority does He teach? To answer
this question, let us go back to a conversation that took place
between God and Moses:

> Then Moses said to God, 'If I come to the people of
> Israel and say to them, "The God of your fathers has
> sent me to you", and they ask me, "What is his name?"
> what shall I say to them?' God said to Moses, 'I AM
> WHO I AM.' And he said, 'Say this to the people of
> Israel, "I AM has sent me to you."'
> (Exodus 3:13-14)

In Hebrew, 'I AM' is written as *eh-yeh*, and comes from the
verb 'to be'. This is God's personal name, conveying His self-
existence, His immortality and His eternal state, in which He
has the authority to be called I AM.

When Jesus came and began to teach, everyone saw a
mortal man of flesh and blood; Rabbi Jesus, son of a
carpenter. There were plenty who tried to discredit Him as a

teacher, but no matter how hard they tried to catch Him out or trip Him up, His teaching was flawless. This caused some to think that maybe He was either the former prophet Elijah or the promised prophet, which is what was also asked about John the Baptiser. This came from the Scriptures, which say:

> I will raise up for them a prophet like you from among their brothers. And I will put my words in his mouth, and he shall speak to them all that I command him. (Deuteronomy 18:18)

> Behold, I will send you Elijah the prophet before the great and awesome day of the LORD comes. (Malachi 4:5)

Jesus knew the expectancy of the people for their Messiah to come and save them, but instead of identifying Himself as such and declaring, 'Behold your Saviour, Immanuel, the Anointed One, now stands among you,' He chose to identify Himself in a slightly more subtle way. The thing that I find most fascinating is that Jesus chose seven 'I AM' statements as His credentials.

I am the bread of life

John 6 begins with the miracle feeding of the five thousand from a simple lunch, given by a kind and thoughtful young boy. After this, Jesus spent some time alone before making His way to Capernaum, where the crowd found Him the next day. He knew they had only sought Him out because He had fed them, so He urged them, 'Do not labour for the food that perishes, but for the food that endures to eternal life, which the Son of Man will give to you. For on him God the Father has set his seal' (John 6:27). Jesus was trying to get them to see beyond their immediate physical needs to their spiritual need. The people asked what labour they needed to do in order to do the works of God, for which the answer was simply to believe in the one that God had sent.[11] The people were not completely satisfied with that answer and wanted Him to perform in order to prove Himself. It just amazes me that after they had witnessed thousands receive their fill of food not twenty-four hours previously, they wanted more signs. They even referred to Moses giving their ancestors bread from heaven, which Jesus quickly corrected by pointing out that it was God who provided the bread, not Moses. He continued to explain that the bread that God provides 'gives life to the world' (John 6:33). So, they said to Him:

'Sir, give us this bread always.'
Jesus said to them, 'I am the bread of life; whoever comes to me shall not hunger.'
(John 6:34-35)

Unfortunately, the people were not the only ones who got distracted by their physical needs; the disciples also worried about food. On one particular day, they were discussing the fact that they had no bread, even though they actually had one loaf between them. Now, let me ask you, if you had witnessed Jesus feeding five thousand people with five loaves and two fish and then on a separate occasion watched Him feed four thousand people with seven loaves and a few small fish,[12] would you really be concerned that one loaf wouldn't feed thirteen of you? What was it that they just couldn't grasp? Did they maybe feel that the miracles were for the benefit of others but not for them, that somehow their needs were not a factor? Or were they simply fixated on this one moment when they were hungry men with one loaf of bread? The Lord cuts in on their conversation, asking, 'Having eyes do you not see, and having ears do you not hear? And do you not remember?' (Mark 8:18).

---

[11] John 6:29.
[12] Mark 8:1-9.

We don't know how Jesus was feeling when He spoke to the disciples that day. Was He frustrated or was He just sad? He was the bread of life; He was everything they would ever need. They were just as important to Him as anyone in the crowd, and yet they still didn't fully understand this truth. Do we grasp this truth fully ourselves and do we always see Jesus for who He truly is?

In the person of Jesus, God had once again sent down His manna from heaven, only this time it was not to feed the body, but the soul. Food is a necessity of daily life and we need a certain amount on a regular basis as physical fuel; without it, the body will slowly shut down. Likewise, as Christians we need God's Word as nourishment to fuel the spiritual body, for it points us to the bread that we cannot do without.

Never stop craving God's Word and let it feed your soul always, for it will strengthen you and sustain you every day.

I am the light of the world

This aspect of the person of Jesus was prophesied in both the Old and New Testaments. Isaiah proclaimed many times about the coming of God's chosen one, but the focus in chapters 9 and 60 is directed towards Jesus as the light:

> The people who walked in darkness
> have seen a great light;
> those who dwelt in a land of deep darkness,
> on them has light shined.
> (Isaiah 9:2)

> Arise, shine, for your light has come,
> and the glory of the LORD has risen upon you.
> (Isaiah 60:1)

In the New Testament we have the wonderful prophecy of Zechariah who, after being made mute for nine months, was released from silence following the birth of his son, John, and spoke these words:

> Because of the tender mercy of our God,
> whereby the sunrise shall visit us from on high
> to give light to those who sit in darkness and in the shadow of death,
> to guide our feet into the way of peace.
> (Luke 1:78-79)

What beautiful imagery Zechariah portrays concerning the Messiah, seeing Him as the sun, heralding in the dawn of a new day filled with hope. The Lord Himself was coming down to walk among His people, to give light to those who sit in darkness and to remove the fear of death. The God who spoke light into existence looked down upon a darkened earth and chose the time to send a new light into the world; a living light.

The God of mercy, who 'commanded the morning since [the] days began, and caused the dawn to know its place' (Job 38:12), was sending forth 'the sun of righteousness' which would 'rise with healing in its wings' (Malachi 4:2); a sun that would never be eclipsed.

Jesus was sent to be the living light among the people, helping them to clearly see the path that leads to abundant life. Jesus declared Himself as the light, saying, 'I am the light of the world. Whoever follows me will not walk in darkness, but will have the light of life' (John 8:12). The devil is the one who has brought the darkness into this world, and he lures people to walk in his ways, but the darkness can never hold back the dawn, and nothing could ever hold back the birth of the Saviour; the light of the world.

I am the door

The third and fourth statements of identity – the door and the good shepherd – are provided alongside each other in

John 10 and both give an understanding of the shepherd's protective relationship with his sheep. After a day in the fields, the flock would be brought together and led into a stone enclosure. Once they were all safely inside, the shepherd would place himself at the opening to the fold. This is where he stayed; this is where he slept. He was, quite literally, the door:

> I am the door. If anyone enters by me, he will be saved
> and will go in and out and find pasture.
> (John 10:9)

The shepherd ensured that his sheep were safe from danger by guarding them with his own life. In the morning, he would lead them out from the enclosure, and, 'When he has brought out all his own, he goes before them, and the sheep follow him' (John 10:4). Again, the safety of the sheep is at the forefront, for they are not just let loose to wander and roam wherever they like. The shepherd goes before them, looking for potential dangers, and leads them to fresh pasture. The shepherd's only concern is the care and welfare of his flock, and he tends to them continually.

Jesus is the door to the fold. Anyone who goes through that door is enclosed in safety, for the Lord has said, 'he will be saved'. The Greek word for saved is *sōthēsetai*, which means save, preserve, heal, rescue, deliver, protect. This is such a beautiful description of the care we receive and a wonderful assurance to all those who have responded to the call of Jesus. Our welfare is always at the forefront of His mind. Always has been, and always will be.

Each day the Lord goes before us, and through the darkest of times He encloses us in safety. He neither slumbers nor sleeps,[13] in order that we can do so in peace.

---

[13] Psalm 121:4.

I am the good shepherd

Jesus presented Himself as a shepherd, primarily because it was a concept that the people of the day could relate to very easily. He also used this visual representation because of the nature of sheep themselves. There appears to be a misconception that sheep are not overly intelligent, but those who rear them and research them will tell you that they are intelligent, emotional and complex animals.[14] That being said, they cannot care for themselves completely and need someone to look out for them and lead them.

The most famous shepherd of the Bible is probably David, which was the job he had before becoming king of Israel. David's knowledge of shepherding is used in his beautiful poem of Psalm 23, and it gives us a better understanding of the relationship between the shepherd and the sheep:

> The LORD is my shepherd; I shall not want.
> He makes me lie down in green pastures.
> He leads me beside still waters.
> He restores my soul.
> He leads me in paths of righteousness
> for his name's sake.
> Even though I walk through the valley of the shadow
> of death,
> I will fear no evil,
> for you are with me;
> your rod and your staff,
> they comfort me.
> You prepare a table before me
> in the presence of my enemies;
> you anoint my head with oil;
> my cup overflows.
> Surely goodness and mercy shall follow me

---

[14] www.wellbeingintlstudiesrepository.org/animsent/vol4/iss25/1/ (accessed 14th April 2024).

all the days of my life,
and I shall dwell in the house of the LORD
for ever.

The shepherd invests his time and energy into the complete care of his flock. He makes sure they have good pasture to feed on and clean water to drink, as well as watching over those who wander and ensuring that they stay clear of danger.

As Jesus speaks of being the good shepherd, the words He uses are full of hope and love, alongside words of caution, warning us to be careful who we trust and who we follow. He tells us, 'He who does not enter the sheepfold by the door but climbs in by another way, that man is a thief and a robber' (John 10:1). Jesus teaches that we should be aware of those who claim to love the Lord but seem only to bring discord and division among God's people. Those who cause strife and discontentment will rob us of our unity in Christ. The only way to combat this is to know the voice of the Saviour: 'My sheep hear my voice, and I know them, and they follow me' (John 10:27).

When we study God's Word and listen to the teachings of Jesus, we get to know His voice. Then, when someone else comes along and tries to lead us in a different direction, we will recognise the voice to be untrue. The good shepherd knows each of His sheep by name, and as He calls them, leads them and guides them, they follow, because they know the sound of His voice: 'I am the good shepherd. I know my own and my own know me' (John 10:14).

All those who respond to the call of Jesus are brought into the fold. The children of Israel may have been God's chosen people from the beginning, but Jesus informs the Jews:

> I have other sheep that are not of this fold. I must bring them also, and they will listen to my voice. So there will be one flock, one shepherd.
> (John 10:16)

Over the years the flock has become divided and the Christian religion has diverged into many different denominations. Division inevitably comes when we listen to our own voice above that of the Lord. However, although we have divided ourselves into different groups, like sheep living in different fields, through Jesus we are one flock, and He is the one shepherd over all.

All those who have come into the care of the good shepherd will be given constant attention and provision, for there is nothing that the shepherd will not do for His sheep:

> I am the good shepherd. The good shepherd lays
> down his life for the sheep.
> (John 10:11)

Through faith, we trust in His unfailing love to sustain and strengthen us in every season of life. His goodness and mercy are renewed daily, and those of us who follow Him have been granted full access to it.

Come what may, through good days and bad, the presence of God never leaves us, and at the end of our days, when the sun goes down, we will 'dwell in the house of the LORD for ever'.

I am the resurrection and the life

Jesus received word that someone very dear to Him was sick; his name was Lazarus and he was the brother of Martha and Mary. The sisters sent a messenger to inform Jesus that Lazarus was ill. There was no pleading for Jesus to come quickly, just the facts of the situation. They knew that the Lord loved them, they knew that He had the ability to heal their brother, and in their hearts they both had the expectation that He would do so.

Jesus waited two days after receiving the message from Martha and Mary before making the journey to Bethany. In all things, Jesus followed the will of the Father because there was (and always is) a bigger picture to be revealed. Jesus knew that the glory of God was to be shown through this event, 'that the Son of God may be glorified through it' (John 11:4). God's timing is perfect; He knows exactly what needs to be done and when. It won't always look like that to us, but that is where faith comes in.

As soon as Martha heard that Jesus was close by, she went out to meet Him while Mary remained at home. The story in Luke 10:38-42 shows us that the sisters had different personalities, and here in John 11 we see two different interactions with Jesus. Martha approached, face to face, not with anger but with a gentle strength, a steadfast faith and quiet sorrow. She said, 'Lord, if you had been here, my brother would not have died. But even now I know that whatever you ask from God, God will give you' (John 11:21-22). Jesus replied:

> I am the resurrection and the life. Whoever believes in me, though he die, yet shall he live, and everyone who lives and believes in me shall never die. Do you believe this?
> (John 11:25-26)

Jesus then called for Mary to come to Him, but she could not hide or control her anguish as she fell at His feet, sobbing. Her sorrow was evident and loud and she cried out the same words as her sister: 'Lord, if you had been here, my brother would not have died' (John 11:32). We see the humanity of Jesus played out in this story as we are told that He was 'deeply moved in his spirit and greatly troubled' (John 11:33). He asked where Lazarus was laid and then He wept. Tears flowed from the Saviour, showing His immense compassion, not for the dead, but for the living. Jesus didn't weep for Lazarus, for He knew that the current situation was about to change. Jesus wept alongside Mary and Martha, because He felt the sorrow in their hearts.

The Lord Jesus understands our trials and our sorrows; He knows the turmoil and tragedy that we endure within this broken world. He *feels* our pain because He *bore* our pain, by taking it upon Himself and carrying it to the cross. This is not the world that the Lord created for us and it breaks His heart. Reassuringly for us, there is no situation that He cannot work through, and He will always work for the good of those who love Him.[15]

The story of Lazarus is not about death; it is about life. The glorious hope is that the death of this earthly, physical body cannot and will not extinguish the life we have in Christ:

> Truly, truly, I say to you, whoever hears my word and believes him who sent me has eternal life. He does not come into judgement, but has passed from death to life.
> (John 5:24)

Notice the tense 'has passed'. This tells us that from the moment we believe, death no longer has any power because we now possess everlasting life in Jesus our Saviour. This is why the apostle Paul could repeat with absolute confidence, 'O death, where is your victory? O death, where is your sting?' (1 Corinthians 15:55).

In John 11:26 we hear Jesus rephrase the truth of life and death as He says, 'Everyone who lives and believes in me shall never die.' And then He finishes with a question: 'Do you believe this?' Jesus is asking the question because believing is the key. We can hear the truth and debate the truth, but nothing changes until we actually believe the truth of Jesus Christ, the Son of God. It is this belief in Jesus that brings us comfort in our sorrow, hope in our trials, and ultimately gives us life over death.

---

15 Romans 8:28.

I am the way, and the truth, and the life

For me, the most important truth of the Bible is found in this verse:

> For there is one God, and there is one mediator
> between God and men, the man Christ Jesus.
> (1 Timothy 2:5)

It is, in fact, a parcel of truths because it contains more than one. First, there is *one* God, and second, there is only one access point to the one God. Regardless of what the world thinks or tries to convince us of, there are not 'many paths' that lead to God. There is one and one alone, 'the man Christ Jesus'. Jesus said:

> I am the way, and the truth, and the life. No one
> comes to the Father except through me.
> (John 14:6)

He didn't say, 'I am a way,' or, 'I am one of many ways.' He said, I am *the* way, the only way, which is how He has the authority to say, 'No one comes to the Father except through me.' There is no other possible way for sinful people to be reconciled to a holy God than through the death of Jesus, and it is the desire of God the Father that all people come to know this truth.[16]

Jesus came not only to show the way back to the Father, but also to be the way; the way of redemption. The only path we can take to achieve a restored union with God is through Jesus. When we try to achieve it through an alternative way, then the death of Jesus becomes meaningless and without purpose. The life of Jesus was all about purpose, divine purpose, and the world has never seen anything more

---

[16] 1 Timothy 2:4.

meaningful than the death of Jesus Christ, Son of Man, Son of God.

Jesus is our mediator and advocate before Almighty God, and through Christ alone we are given access to the throne room and mercy seat of the Father.

I am the true vine

This is the seventh and final revelation of Jesus regarding His 'I AM' nature. There were vineyards far and wide in Galilee, as they were a big part of their economy, as well as their diet, and this was an image that everyone could relate to. Through the symbol of the vine, Jesus wanted His disciples and followers to understand that the only path to productive growth was through Him. He was the life source, and everything they needed stemmed from Him. As long as they remained in Him, they would bear fruit, but attached to this there was a warning:

> Every branch in me that does not bear fruit he takes away, and every branch that does bear fruit he prunes, that it may bear more fruit.
> (John 15:2)

As followers of Christ, we too have been grafted into the true vine and everything we need for this earthly life stems from Him. As long as we remain in Him, we will continue to grow and have productive Christian lives. Sometimes, though, it will feel like we are doing the right thing, we are on the right path and everything is good, when all of a sudden, the ground shakes and we lose our footing. During those times, it can be hard to understand what went wrong. It is possible, even likely, that we did nothing wrong. God just got the shears out, and pruning can be ruthless. God sees the fruit our lives are producing and knows that we have so much more to give. He cuts a little, maybe even a lot, back, to encourage more growth, because He wants us to flourish. So we shouldn't get downhearted when it feels like things are changing; rather, we should get excited about what God has in store for the next part of the journey:

> By this my Father is glorified, that you bear much fruit
> and so prove to be my disciples.
> (John 15:8)

The lesson of the vine came near the end of Jesus' ministry which, for the disciples, meant that their time of sitting at the feet of their teacher was drawing to a close. Their literal baptism by fire was approaching and they would soon have to stand on the truth of His teachings without His physical presence to guide and direct them. A new guide and helper was waiting, and these tender saplings that Jesus had grafted into the vine would grow and mature.

We need this same growth in maturity, and it is the Holy Spirit who helps us to develop strong branches and encourages us in producing good fruit. If we do not keep ourselves firmly attached to the vine, we become a branch that withers, and there is no glory to be found in dead leaves. We need to remain in Jesus, living productive lives that bring glory to Him and to the Father.

Knowing who He is

The Ancient of Days, Eternal God, Alpha and Omega – these are just a few of the names that define God the Father, God the Spirit and God the Son, which gave Jesus the authority to describe Himself through these wonderful 'I AM' statements, for He also declared, 'I and the Father are one' (John 10:30).

The one theme that runs through all of these beautiful descriptions is life; the glorious hope of life in Christ, both here on earth and then with Him for all eternity. He shines a light in the darkness that we might find the path back to God. He provides us with manna for the journey and spiritual sustenance for productive and abundant lives. He encloses us in safety and protects us with His own life. He provides all that we need here and now, and then leads us to everlasting life with Him. Jesus brings Life; Jesus gives Life; Jesus is Life.

Knowing who it is we serve and why we serve Him is fundamental to our faith. We need to know and understand why we follow His commands and why we live our lives according to His teaching. Our obedience to God and our faith in Jesus are grounded in the truth of who He is, what He has done and what He continues to do on our behalf:

> Know therefore today, and lay it to your heart, that the LORD is God in heaven above and on the earth beneath; there is no other.
> (Deuteronomy 4:39)

It does our spirit good to meditate on this truth, that the One we serve is the one true God. It is our choice to serve Him; it is our choice to follow Him, and it is our choice to commit to Him. In the next couple of chapters, we will look at the different aspects of faith: the choice, the cost, the commitment and the continual process of following Jesus. We may have already made our choice, but it is good for us to reaffirm in our own hearts and minds why we live our lives for Him. In understanding the call of the Saviour and the conviction of the Holy Spirit in our own lives, we can better explain to others about the need for a personal response of their own.

Reflections

Questions

- Jesus uses various symbols to help us understand who He is, as well as who we are in relation to Him. Which of these do you find most helpful in understanding this unique relationship?

- How sure are you of your importance to God, and how confident are you that He will always provide for your needs?

- As you grow as a Christian, what kind of 'good fruit' ('love, joy, peace, patience, kindness, goodness, faithfulness, gentleness, self-control', Galatians 5:22-23) can you see growing and developing in your life? Are there any that you struggle with that you could perhaps talk to someone about?

Practical application

Read Psalm 23 and make a list of all the places where the Lord is with His sheep, and what He does for them in each place. Think about what each place might represent in your life, and write down what the Lord can do for you in each of these situations.

Prayer

Thank You, Lord, for showing me who You are and for helping me to realise who I am, both in You and to You. I need You to light the path ahead of me and I am thankful that You walk beside me every step of the way. Thank You for providing for all of my needs and for caring about every aspect of my life. I want to bring You glory in all that I do, so help me to grow in You and to live a life that produces good fruit. Amen.

3
Faith is your choice

For God so loved the world, that he gave his only Son,
that whoever believes in him should not perish but
have eternal life.
(John 3:16)

Life is full of choices: Which music to listen to, where to shop, what to have for breakfast? Watch a programme or read a book; go for a walk or a run; ask for help or go it alone? We make thousands of choices on a daily basis. In fact, according to the website Psychology Today, the average adult is estimated to make around 35,000 of them![17] Some will be important and some won't; some will be of no consequence and others will have the ability to change our life completely. One such choice is whether to put our faith in God: 'choose this day whom you will serve' (Joshua 24:15).

A choice in believing

The first step of faith comes with acknowledging the sovereignty of God and believing that the Bible is His true Word. It is the acceptance that Jesus is the Son of God, born of a virgin, who lived to show us the way to the Father and

---

[17] www.psychologytoday.com/us/blog/stretching-theory/201809/how-many-decisions-do-we-make-each-day (accessed 15th April 2024).

died to pay the price of our sin. It is believing and accepting that Jesus is the Father's wonderful gift of salvation. It is believing that He rose again on the third day, showing that death has no victory, but is simply the doorway to the believer's eternal home in heaven.

For each of us, our journey of faith begins with a response, just like that of the disciples:

> While walking by the Sea of Galilee, he saw two brothers, Simon (who is called Peter) and Andrew his brother, casting a net into the sea, for they were fishermen. And he said to them, 'Follow me, and I will make you fishers of men.' Immediately they left their nets and followed him.
> (Matthew 4:18-20)

This was the call to the first two disciples, Andrew and Simon, who lived in Bethsaida. Andrew was expectant of the Messiah's arrival because, up until this point, he had been a disciple of John the Baptiser. He had also brought his brother Simon to meet Jesus previously (John 1:40-42). So when Jesus called to them on the shore that day, they knew exactly who He was and there was no hesitation at all, for, '*Immediately* they left their nets and followed him' (Matthew 4:20, my emphasis). This same scenario was also true for James and his brother John. For Matthew himself, the only difference in the calling was the setting. When Jesus called to him, Matthew was 'sitting at the tax booth, and [Jesus] said to him, "Follow me." And he rose and followed him' (Matthew 9:9).

As a rabbi, Jesus acquired many followers during His time of ministry, in addition to the twelve He had personally called. There were lots of lessons that He would give and a lot of imagery that He would use in order to explain the teachings in the Scriptures, as well as the truth of who He was. On one such occasion, after He had spoken in the synagogue regarding the bread of life, a lot of the followers were left feeling very confused because they didn't understand the symbolic nature of Jesus' body and blood.[18] Although Jesus was indeed seen by some as a great teacher, or even a prophet of God, they still only recognised Him as the son of Joseph. They were disturbed about the reference to His Father and that He Himself had come down as bread from heaven. They grumbled among themselves, asking who could possibly listen to this kind of talk?

Even though Jesus tried to change their perception from a literal interpretation of His words to a spiritual one, it was still too much for some, and, 'After this many of his disciples turned back and no longer walked with him' (John 6:66). Sadly for some, when choosing to follow meant choosing to believe, they had in fact been following the crowd, and not Jesus Himself. Jesus was looking for those who truly believed in who He was, which was why He turned to the twelve and asked:

> 'Do you want to go away as well?' Simon Peter answered him, 'Lord, to whom shall we go? You have the words of eternal life, and we have believed, and have come to know, that you are the Holy One of God.'
> (John 6:67-69)

Following Jesus is a personal choice, a choice that is made through believing. We either believe that Jesus is the Son of God or we believe that He was just a great teacher or prophet, and that belief triggers a decision. Simon Peter recognised his own need and that Jesus was the only one who was offering a different kind of life, a different way of living. It was deeper and richer, and it took him beyond what he felt physically. His spirit was alive and he knew without a shadow of a doubt that Jesus had awakened him with words of eternal life.

---

[18] John 6:22-71.

Think back to what it was that awakened your spirit and led you to follow Jesus. What was it about Him that made you answer His call?

When I was very young, the phrase 'called of God' usually went hand in hand with those in missionary service across the world, so in my mind, being 'called' meant going somewhere very far away. As a little girl, that frightened me somewhat as I wondered, 'Where will God send me? Will I be able to go where He tells me? What if I go to the wrong place?' Tough questions for such a young mind. As I got older, I learned (much to my relief) that God's 'call' could be to do a whole variety of things; He was simply calling me to follow and I simply had to trust where He would lead.

One of the exciting parts of following is in the discovery of what God knows we are capable of doing, because it usually pushes the boundaries of what we imagine that to be. Did I think that I would write songs and be invited to sing in different churches across the country? No, far too scary. Did I ever imagine that I would write a book and that people would actually be reading it? Absolutely not. As apprehensive as I was in both of these things, though, I trusted God's direction and discovered how exciting it is to embark on new ventures and uncover new possibilities.

A life lived for God is never boring, for it is a life full of purpose and adventure. When Jesus says, 'Follow Me,' He wants us to trust Him completely. Has He been calling you lately? Have you felt a pull in a certain direction but fear and uncertainty are holding you back? Don't dismiss what He puts on your heart to do, no matter how small or how big you think it is. He may not be calling you to go across the world, but He might be calling you to go across the street and check on a neighbour, or drop a card through their letterbox. A small gesture can have a huge impact. So when Jesus says, 'Go and do,' there should be no hesitation; just like the man in the next story.

A personal choice

John 9 tells the incredible story of a man born blind who was healed by Jesus and then cast out by the Pharisees. All those who knew the blind man were in no doubt that it was a miracle, but he had to retell his story over and over. The Pharisees were once again putting on a display of sanctimonious offence because the healing had taken place on the Sabbath. When they asked the man for a second time what had happened, he told them that the story hadn't changed from the first time they asked. This was his testimony: 'The man called Jesus made mud and anointed my eyes and said to me, "Go to Siloam and wash." So I went and washed and received my sight' (John 9:11).

The Pharisees were incensed when the man went on to ask them if they wanted to become Jesus' disciples. As far as they were concerned, they were disciples of Moses, so why would they want to follow someone whose origin was unknown? This was the man's incredible response:

> Why, this is an amazing thing! You do not know where he comes from, and yet he opened my eyes ... if anyone is a worshipper of God and does his will, God listens to him. Never since the world began has it been heard that anyone opened the eyes of a man born blind. If this man were not from God, he could do nothing.
> (John 9:30-33)

Refusing to accept the truth and refusing to be taught by a 'sinner', they threw the man out of the synagogue. Having never seen the one who healed him, the man did not recognise Jesus when He came and stood before him once more. Jesus asked him if he believed in the Son of Man, to which he confessed that he didn't know who that person was:

> Jesus said to him, 'You have seen him, and it is he who is speaking to you.' He said, 'Lord, I believe,' and he worshipped him.
> (John 9:37-38)

In overhearing this conversation, some of the Pharisees then asked Jesus if they too were blind. Jesus' reply would not be well received: 'If you were blind, you would have no guilt; but now that you say, "We see", your guilt remains' (John 9:41). All those who had seen and heard Jesus were now accountable for their sin and, regardless of the opinions of others, a choice had to be made to either believe or not believe.

Every lesson that Jesus teaches comes with a personal choice. Opinions about what Jesus teaches will vary greatly and some voices will be very loud indeed, especially if it is in opposition. However, the decision to accept what He says and to follow Him is ours alone to make, and it is something that we must continually choose to do.

A personal belief

No matter how often Jesus proclaimed the gospel of the kingdom, the Jewish people still asked Him, 'If you are the Christ, tell us plainly' (John 10:24). True scholars of the Scriptures, who knew and understood the prophecies, accepted Jesus as the awaited Messiah. Their hearts and minds were open to the truth, so that when Jesus spoke, they heard the voice of God. The religious leaders, however, were so caught up in their own power and self-righteousness that they remained spiritually blind to the truth. No matter what Jesus said, they refused to listen. It is true that anyone could have said they were the Messiah, but Jesus was the only one with the ability to display the power of the kingdom. He had returned strength to the lame, hearing to the deaf, sight to the blind and healing to the broken, and brought forgiveness to the sinner. He had taken the food of one and fed thousands, which is why he asked them to believe the works, if not the words:

> Even though you do not believe me, believe the works, that you may know and understand that the Father is in me and I am in the Father.
> (John 10:38)

Those who are intent on going their own way and who boast that they are masters of their own destiny are sadly being led by the master of deceit, who takes great pleasure in their blindness. Those in search of the truth will find Jesus.

Faith is a personal choice to believe the words and the works of Jesus; to respond to His call and commit to following His path. It is not an easy path, for it is narrow and it can be difficult. Jesus is very clear in His teachings regarding the cost and commitment involved in being His disciple (which we will look at in the next chapter), and although He wants to prepare us for that, the main reason for discussing it is for reassurance. He wants us to know that He is with us every step of the way and that we walk in His strength. When we stand for Him, He stands for us, and when Jesus is for us, the enemy has more to fear than we do.

Reflections

Questions

- You cannot completely block out the opinions of others, but you can choose whether or not to let them overwhelm you. What can you do to ensure that you are following the voice of Jesus and not the voice of the crowd?

- Have you been aware of the Lord calling you in a certain direction? What thoughts and feelings have you experienced, and are you ready to be taken on a new adventure?

- How did it feel the first time you shared your faith, or the first time you told someone you had become a Christian?

Practical application
As you talk to God, ask Him to lead you towards something practical that you can do – then listen carefully. God will speak and He will do it in a variety of ways. He may show you through a verse, or present a volunteering opportunity, or simply bring someone to your mind.

Prayer
Lord, help me to listen to Your voice above all others and to go where You are leading. I want to discover all the things that You know I am capable of doing, so help me to push the boundaries of what I think I can do. I want a life full of purpose and adventure with You. Lead me. I will follow. Amen.

4

The cost and commitment of faith

I have prayed for you that your faith may not fail.
(Luke 22:32)

Faith has a cost

As the weeks and months went by, the disciples soon
discovered that following Jesus was not always plain sailing.
This was confirmed to them when Jesus said, 'If anyone
would come after me, let him deny himself and take up his
cross daily and follow me' (Luke 9:23). For the Christian
today, when we think of the cross, our thoughts are of God's
love and Christ's sacrifice, but what it would have conjured
up in the minds of the disciples and the other Jewish people
of the time was something entirely different. It was not
unlikely that some among them had relatives or friends who
had been crucified by the Roman governor Varus. Following
an uprising of the Jews in Galilee and Judea (around 4 BC),
the Romans called in the help of Varus, who arrived with two
legions of soldiers. He quelled the revolt, crucified
approximately two thousand Jews and lined the roads of
Galilee with the crosses as a warning.[19] So for the people who
heard Jesus speaking that day, the cross was a symbol of
horrific punishment and death.

---

[19] William Whiston, *The Complete Works of Flavius Josephus* (Green Forest,
AZ: Master Books, 2008), p 418.

Picture that as you listen to Jesus say, 'whoever does not take his cross and follow me is not worthy of me' (Matthew 10:38). The Zealots (extremely patriotic Jews who advocated to overthrow Roman rule and were among those at the forefront of the revolt) would go to any lengths to maintain the integrity of the Jewish nation against Roman paganism. In denying oneself, you had to be willing to abandon all personal safeguards. There was a cost involved in following Jesus, and in AD 27 that would have been all too clear. It took true faith to believe that Jesus was indeed the long-awaited Messiah, and it took true commitment to follow His teaching. Jesus was clear about the cost, saying, 'For whoever is ashamed of me and of my words, of him will the Son of Man be ashamed' (Luke 9:26).

I am committed to Jesus Christ as Lord and I am not ashamed for anyone to know that, but then, I am privileged not to be living in fear of persecution (unlike many Christians across the world today who suffer greatly for their faith). Back then it was hard enough being a Jew, but to be a Jewish follower of Rabbi Jesus meant that you were living with a target on your back. Their commitment, though, was fuelled by the hope of His promise that 'everyone who acknowledges me before men, the Son of Man also will acknowledge before the angels of God' (Luke 12:8).

Being willing to relinquish the temporal things of earth, even your own life, for the eternal glories of God's kingdom is the definition of a true disciple of Jesus.

The truth, of course, is that even the strongest committed Christian will stumble on occasion. The devil hates seeing strong faith and he loves nothing more than to watch us trip and fall. He looks for any weakness, and then he begins to pull on that thread. Even the disciples, with Jesus alongside them, would not be immune to the testing of their faith. Jesus warned Simon Peter of this:

> Simon, Simon, behold, Satan demanded to have you,
> that he might sift you like wheat, but I have prayed for
> you that your faith may not fail. And when you have
> turned again, strengthen your brothers.
> (Luke 22:31-32)

When you read through the four Gospels, you get a picture of the character of Simon: a physically strong man, full of confidence who acted a lot on impulse. Satan was about to test this bravado and Simon was going to find out what the threshing floor was really like. His self-confidence and strong belief in himself were going to be beaten, shaken and thrown in the air. Have you experienced this? I'm sure you have at one time or another; I know I certainly have, but I now cling to the best part of that verse: 'I have prayed for you.' Oh, to have the Lord on our side, praying for us, interceding on our behalf before the Father.[20] Just pause for a moment and think about that.

Simon, however, is still coasting on his self-confidence, and I imagine him thinking, '*My* faith *fail*? Absolutely not!' So he boldly declares, 'I am ready to go with you both to prison and to death' (Luke 22:33). Sadly, Simon was about to get a real wake-up call. That very day he would deny even knowing Jesus, and he would do it three times. The sifting was about to begin.

Sifting is the process of removing the hard outer shell of the grain to reveal the real substance of the wheat. We all need to go through this process, and it's not easy – in fact, it is usually painful – but we will come out the other side stronger for it. It was a painful experience for Simon, but the Lord knew that he would emerge stronger, and because of it he would be able to help his brothers in Christ.

All that Simon experienced did indeed make him stronger and much bolder for the Lord, which is evident throughout the book of Acts. He also used what he had learned and

---

[20] Romans 8:34.

passed it on to the rest of us. Ironically, or more likely purposely, he reminds all of us to be watchful, with this warning, 'Your adversary the devil prowls around like a roaring lion, seeking someone to devour' (1 Peter 5:8).

So when the trials come that cause us to stumble or fall, we are not to be discouraged. Instead, we learn from them, are strengthened by them and use them to help others along the way, for we will all have to bear our share of trials. However, although Jesus wants us to be aware of challenging times, He wants our focus to remain squarely on Him:

> I have said these things to you, that in me you may
> have peace.
> (John 16:33)

The Lord spoke to His disciples at length on their last evening together, before He was taken to be crucified. There was so much that He wanted to explain to them, and so much that He needed them to understand. They had been with Him for three years and yet they still did not seem to grasp the reality of why He was there, or the events that would unfold. Jesus had spoken about going to prepare a place for them and that He was the Way that they should follow. He tried to reassure them with the promise of the Holy Spirit, who would be with them after He would leave. He had also been very candid in telling them that the world would hate them and there would be persecution. Just as they were trying to get their heads around all that, the Lord reminded them that He was leaving. Imagine how they might be feeling as they tried to process all of this information.

Jesus knew that His disciples were really struggling mentally with what they had heard, but He also felt the ache within them. I have a mental image of them sitting around the Lord with drooping heads as they absorbed the reality of their situation: 'In the world you will have tribulation.' This much truth was not easy to handle. 'But take heart ...' Their drooping heads lifted slightly as they anticipated a flicker of hope. 'I have overcome the world' (John 16:33). Yes, Lord! Amen!

On this narrow path we will have troubles, of that we can be sure. In the middle of it all, remembering who it is we serve, His sacrifice, and the Holy Spirit within us, we can be certain that His promise is true and that in Him we will have peace.

Although it may be difficult at times, the ability to experience peace in spite of our circumstances is what sets the Christian apart. We may be challenged and grieved by various trials, and our faith may be tested often, but this does not extinguish peace. Rather, it leads us to the 'rock of our salvation' (Psalm 95:1). By the power of the Holy Spirit within us, we have an unexplainable internal peace regardless of external circumstances.

This divine peace allows us, as Christians, to retain the joy of salvation through all that this world throws at us. This is because our joy does not come from an earthly perspective but from a heavenly one. We do not rejoice in our grief; we rejoice in the comfort that the Holy Spirit provides. We do not rejoice in our pain; we rejoice in the strength given by God to bear it. We look beyond what is, to what will be.

The Lord Jesus endured the cross 'for the joy that was set before him' (Hebrews 12:2); He didn't rejoice in the agony of the cross but in the glory of the kingdom and His place with the Father. Faith has a cost, but the depth of our peace and fullness of our joy lie in the hope of heaven and our place with the Father, the Son and the Holy Spirit.

Faith requires commitment

Responding to the call of God and understanding the cost of following Him are essential elements of faith. Every day we place ourselves into His hands and commit to trusting His lead, wherever the journey takes us. That's true, isn't it? Think back to when you first decided to follow Jesus. As new Christians we are often full of fire and we long to see what

God has for us, so, like Isaiah we say, 'Here am I! Send me' (Isaiah 6:8). As time goes on, we get more settled, and in the comfortable rhythm of Christian life our response can lose some of the initial enthusiasm: 'Here am I, Lord, send me… but not too far.' For many of us, the older we get, the more settled we become, and we tend to want our commitment to be tailored to *our* needs. The Christian faith, however, is not centred on *our* needs, but on the commands of God.

Abram (later known as Abraham) was seventy-five years old when he was called by God to a new destination. The Lord said to him, 'Go from your country and your kindred and your father's house to the land that I will show you' (Genesis 12:1). Such was his faith and his trust in God that he was willing to uproot his family and embark on an arduous journey from Haran to Canaan. Abram didn't question or hesitate; he just did exactly what the Lord told him.

There is no fulfilment in lukewarm commitment; we are either all in or we're not. God may take us on a literal journey or a spiritual journey, and both may require some upheaval. The Lord wants us to walk with Him wherever the path leads. The question is, do we trust Him enough to lead us out of our own Haran to that better place He has for us?

Before Abram there was another man who didn't question or hesitate to follow God's direction. The book of Genesis tells us of a righteous man with a tremendous, unequivocal faith. His name was Noah and he had 'found favour in the eyes of the LORD' (Genesis 6:8). God told him to build an ark and, without objection, that is exactly what Noah did.

Five years after the death of his father and in the year that his grandfather, Methuselah, died, Noah was the only one found to be blameless in his generation. Noah walked in the will of God and lived according to the word of the Lord. God spoke to Noah and told him that judgement was coming. Although Noah could not see the evidence of it as yet, he believed God's word to be true and followed all that the Lord told him.

When the ark was completed and all the animals were safely on board, Noah and his family went inside, 'And the LORD shut him in' (Genesis 7:16). Everything within the ark was now safe in the refuge of God; their lives were now securely sealed within His promise.

When we walk with God and commit ourselves to fully trust in His Word, we are able to survive the rising waters because we are shut in with Him, under His protection.

Just as Noah's faith *in* God was worked out through his faithfulness *to* God, so too must our faith be worked out through total commitment to the teachings of Jesus and the will of the Father.

Faith is a continual process

Everything about faith is continual. Continual learning; continual growth; continual commitment. Day by day, bit by bit, as we absorb God's Word and the lessons that Jesus taught, we become spiritually stronger as our understanding of what He teaches grows and develops. There are times when we might feel quite strong in our faith, and other times when we possibly feel a bit unsure. There may even be occasions when we imagine that if we had a report card, it would say, 'Could do better.' The truth is, no matter where any of us sit on the scale of faith, we probably feel that it is something we desperately need much more of. This was something that the disciples experienced.

The disciples were with the Lord every day, learning and growing, but as He spoke to them about temptations that would surely come, they felt inadequate in their faith, and they didn't hold back in asking for more. 'The apostles said to the Lord, "Increase our faith!"' (Luke 17:5). Faith is the central part of our salvation and it is pivotal in our daily walk, which is what the disciples themselves were discovering day by day. In answer to their petition, however, the Lord said:

> If you had faith like a grain of mustard seed, you could
> say to this mulberry tree, 'Be uprooted and planted in
> the sea,' and it would obey you.
> (Luke 17:6)

Can you imagine the look of dismay on some faces and the look of concentration on others as they stared at the tree and silently willed it to move, quickly followed by the look of disappointment when not even a leaf fluttered?

The Lord was not trying to discourage them; on the contrary, He was highlighting the fact that faith is not about quantity; it is the substance and depth of faith that makes the difference. A mustard seed, like all types of seed, is small in comparison to what it produces, but the life within the seed will only bear fruit when it is rooted in the correct soil.

The Lord wants us to strive for quality, not quantity. Our seed of faith needs to be tended, nurtured and fed in order for the roots to push deeper and become stronger. This can only be done by listening to Jesus, and continually growing in the lessons that He teaches. The apostle Paul reiterates this:

> Therefore, as you received Christ Jesus the Lord, so
> walk in him, rooted and built up in him and
> established in the faith, just as you were taught,
> abounding in thanksgiving.
> (Colossians 2:6-7)

Do you remember how it felt on the day you decided to lay everything down at the feet of Jesus and accept the Lord into your life? Did it feel like a weight had been lifted off your shoulders? A new beginning, a new way of thinking, a new purpose and direction? Receiving the amazing gift of God's salvation is an incredible feeling and it is a huge first step in the amazing journey of faith. The step of faith then moves forward to become the walk of faith. As we walk, we grow, and good growth comes from strong roots. If you have ever tried to remove a plant or shrub with deep roots, I'm sure you would agree that it is extremely difficult to do. Just think of the humble dandelion, which doesn't look particularly strong from the ground up, but trying to remove it is a whole different story. It actually reminds me of David and Goliath.[21] I imagine that David probably looked like a dandelion in front of a huge rhododendron – the roots of both, however, show a completely different picture.

The building of our faith comes through reading, listening and learning God's Word. As we absorb His truth, our roots grow stronger, and the stronger the roots, the more difficult it will be for the devil to unsettle us. Memorising Scripture, which is 'the sword of the Spirit' (Ephesians 6:17), is an essential weapon in all kinds of situations in daily life, so we should never neglect to study it, allowing it to become a part of us. This will keep our feet on a firm foundation, and we will be blessed when we stay true to it.

In the Gospel of Luke, we read about a particular occasion when Jesus was speaking to a crowd, among which there was a woman who was in awe of His teaching. Unable to contain her adoration, she called out, 'Blessed is the womb that bore you' (Luke 11:27). This was indeed a great compliment for His mother, and it was intended as such, but Jesus did not want the woman to lose the focus of His message, and He immediately redirected her thoughts by saying, 'Blessed rather are those who hear the word of God and keep it!' (Luke 11:28). Jesus was not taking away from the fact that Mary had certainly been blessed by the Father, but He wanted to emphasise to the woman that she herself could receive God's blessing by keeping His Word.

Through the parable of the sower, Jesus describes four scenarios of God's Word being heard and the conditions under which that Word bears fruit.[22] First, there are those who hear but don't understand, and the devil swoops in to take away what they have heard. Next, there are those who

[21] 1 Samuel 17.
[22] Matthew 13:3-9; Mark 4:3-9; Luke 8:5-8.

hear and believe the truth of the Word but fail to become rooted in it, so when trials come, their faith withers. Then there are those who hear the Word but are distracted by the cares of this world, so become blinded to the truth and blessing of living God's way. The final outcome relates to those who hear the Word, understand it, keep it and grow in it, bearing good fruit for all to see. They are the ones who are truly blessed, for they commit to the continual process.

Reading God's Word and listening to God's Word is essential, but it is only the beginning. His Word needs to permeate every fibre of our being, changing our outlook and our attitude towards the things of God, and away from the things of the world. It requires our unwavering focus, and it most definitely requires discipline. Those who are involved in competitive sport or who just try to maintain a healthy lifestyle will understand the concept of both of these things.

The apostle Paul said, 'I do not run aimlessly; I do not box as one beating the air' (1 Corinthians 9:26). Athletes are all completely focused on the task at hand and the achievement of their goal. You don't see runners going in different directions around the track hoping to cross the line at some stage, or running randomly cross-country. You also don't see boxers flailing their arms about in the vain hope of hitting something eventually (well, not all the time). Runners have an agreed starting point and finishing point with a predetermined path in between; boxers know exactly where to land that punch. Each has a target, and that is where their focus lies.

Focus demands discipline and training. Athletes deny their bodies the normal everyday pleasures in order to obtain the condition that is needed to win the ultimate prize. Faith also demands discipline and training in order to be effective in the Christian walk; a walk that is not about competition, but about witness. Like Paul, we do not need to run (or walk) aimlessly. We need to focus our faith and move with conviction and purpose.

Our faith not only strengthens and sustains us for life on the narrow path; it can also encourage those walking alongside us. To walk with a clear purpose can be effective in motivating others to focus on theirs, so don't let it stagnate. Faith is an ever-evolving, living entity which grows stronger as we exercise it. Every day is an opportunity to grow closer to God, and we will benefit greatly if we allow Him to challenge us, excite us and move us into new experiences of who He is. This in turn opens our hearts and minds, allowing the Holy Spirit to set our faith on fire.

Reflections

Questions

- What difference does it make to have the presence of the Lord with you in every situation, and to know that Jesus has 'overcome the world' (John 16:33)?

- Before reading this chapter, were you aware that Jesus is praying for you? How does that make you feel?

- If you have come through a difficult or trying situation in the past, how comfortable do you feel in allowing God to use what you've been through to help someone else?

Practical application
Think of a way that you could be an encouragement to another Christian this week. For example, take them for coffee and find out how they are doing, or send a card, make a phone call or help them with something that needs to be done.

Prayer
Lord, help me to understand Your Word so that my faith can grow deeper and stronger. Challenge me, Lord, and help me to continually experience You in new ways. Set my faith on fire and help me to be an encouragement to those around me. Amen.

5

Faith stories in the Gospels

As we have seen, faith is personal and each of us will come to experience it in a different way. So, to end this group of chapters, we will look at five very different people and think about the faith each displayed in their encounter with Jesus. They are a centurion, a blind man, a Jewish woman, a Canaanite woman and a royal official. These stories are taken from the Gospel accounts with a small serving of personal conjecture as I imagine the scene surrounding these encounters. You may find it helpful to have a Bible beside you for this section, so that you can look more closely at each of these stories.

A centurion: Matthew 8:5-13

> *Lord, I am not worthy to have you come under my roof, but only say the word, and my servant will be healed.*
> *(Matthew 8:8)*

Of all the people most likely to see the truth of who Jesus was, a Roman centurion would probably not be at the top of most people's list. How it happened we do not know, but somehow his eyes had been opened. Rabbi Jesus was becoming very well known because He didn't just teach at

His local synagogue but travelled constantly throughout the whole province.

The centurion in our story lived in Capernaum, which is also where Jesus lived after leaving Nazareth, so he definitely would have heard about Him, but it had to be more personal than that. He must have heard Jesus with his own ears and had his heart opened to the truth by the power of the Holy Spirit. When his servant became sick, he knew there was only one who could help. Perhaps he hadn't seen the teacher about for a while so he asked around and left instructions that as soon as anyone caught sight of Him, they were to come and inform him immediately.

When Jesus arrived back in Capernaum, the centurion wasted no time in coming and appealing to Him, 'Lord, my servant is lying paralysed at home, suffering terribly'. Jesus agreed to come and heal him, but the soldier said no: 'I am not worthy to have you come under my roof'. He told Jesus that he understood authority, both having it and being under it, so all he required of the Lord was for Him to say the word. Jesus marvelled at his faith, saying, 'Truly, I tell you, with no one in Israel have I found such faith'. Then turning to the soldier He said, 'Go; let it be done for you as you have believed.'

'As you have believed' – a Roman centurion displayed to all those following Jesus, including the disciples, what it meant to have a believing faith. More than that, he let all those around him see what it meant to exercise that faith, showing the substance of it – just like the lesson of the mustard seed.

In considering the faith of the centurion, it's good to pause and ask ourselves, in what way are we exercising our faith? Do we bring all of our circumstances to Jesus? The truth is, we don't tend to bring *every* situation to God – at least not at first – but over time that changes. We come to realise that He really is interested in every aspect of our lives and He wants us to bring it all to Him. He wants us to come believing.

A blind man: Mark 10:46-52

And when he heard that it was Jesus of Nazareth, he began to cry out and say, 'Jesus, Son of David, have mercy on me!'
(Mark 10:47)

Jesus and His disciples had spent time in Jericho, spreading the gospel to all who would listen. It was now time to leave and head towards Jerusalem. As was now customary, a crowd was following Jesus on His way. An early start was most likely required as it was approximately a seven-hour walk, the majority of which was uphill. They would need to rest at midday from the heat of the sun and replenish their waterbags; then hopefully arrive before evening... if there were no distractions.

It seems Bartimaeus had heard the teacher speak and was convinced that He was the Messiah. Unfortunately, because he was blind, he had been unable to get close to Jesus; there were always so many people around Him. He heard that Jesus was leaving the town the next morning and knew that he only had one more chance to get His attention. So he rose early, got himself by the side of the road, perhaps close to the city gate, and waited.

He knew by the chatter and commotion that Jesus was coming his way. Afraid of missing his opportunity he began to cry out, 'Jesus, Son of David, have mercy on me!' Some people began telling him to be quiet and not to bother the teacher. Bartimaeus would not be deterred and, raising his voice even louder, cried, 'Son of David, have mercy on me!' Then we read, 'And Jesus stopped.' The fact that he used the name 'Son of David' convinces me that Bartimaeus believed that Jesus was indeed the promised Messiah. His faith in this belief was so strong that nothing was going to stand in his way.

Jesus responded by calling him to come. Bartimaeus did not need to be asked twice, for 'throwing off his cloak, he sprang up and came to Jesus'. What a scene as people moved out of his way to let him through, eager now themselves to see what would unfold. Focused on Bartimaeus alone, Jesus said to him:

> 'What do you want me to do for you?' And the blind man said to him, 'Rabbi, let me recover my sight.' And Jesus said to him, 'Go your way; your faith has made you well.' And immediately he recovered his sight and followed him on the way.
> (Mark 10:51-52)

He knew this was the Messiah and his faith had prevailed. The world had been opened up to him and Rabbi Jesus had told him he was now able to go on his way. Bartimaeus knew that there was only one way he wanted to go, and that was wherever Jesus was going. From the moment Jesus touched his life, he followed Him.

My favourite three words in this story are, 'And Jesus stopped' – words that are as incredible as they are beautiful. When we call out to Jesus, He hears us and He asks, 'What do you want me to do for you?' At some point in our lives, we will more than likely find ourselves in a situation that requires a miracle. Like Bartimaeus, we may need to be persistent in calling out to Jesus, but of this we can be sure – Jesus always hears those who call upon His name, and He still responds to those who believe.

And he said to the woman, 'Your faith has saved you;
go in peace.'
(Luke 7:50)

Jesus had been invited to eat at the home of a Pharisee named Simon. It appears his invitation did not come from a place of honesty or sincerity, but was more for show to prove that Jesus was a fraud in one way or another. He certainly had no genuine respect for Jesus as he did not greet Him as a friend or peer, or even as a proper guest. There was no kiss on the cheek, no water for His feet and no oil for His head; the customary traditions of a hospitable host had purposely been omitted. This was nothing short of insulting.

Among those present at Simon's home was a woman who had found forgiveness through Jesus, forgiveness that she never imagined was even possible, forgiveness that she knew she didn't deserve. Nevertheless, she had received redemption from God, so the love and joy that she felt were immeasurable. She heard that Jesus had been invited to eat at the home of the Pharisee and she didn't want to miss the opportunity to express her heartfelt thanks to the one who had changed her life.

She brought perfume with her, probably to anoint His hands after they had been washed, but that had not happened. Instead, her Lord had been humiliated. Now He reclined, unwashed, at the table, and it seems she could not help but weep at the indignity being imposed upon Him. Jesus' feet were soaked with her tears; having no towel, she loosened her hair and used it to dry them. She kissed them, showing Him personal respect, and then anointed them with the perfume to show her immense gratitude.

Simon felt justified in his treatment of Jesus because, if He really was a prophet, then surely He would know what kind of woman sat before Him? Simon's first mistake was in judging the woman to still be a sinner, so Jesus took the opportunity to tell him a parable about a moneylender and two debtors. Simon's second mistake was not recognising himself or the woman in this story as the ones who were in debt. Hopefully, through this encounter, Simon did not make a more costly mistake by failing to acknowledge his own sin and receiving the forgiveness being offered.

In order that no one else would make the same mistake in misjudging this woman, Jesus turned and said to her, 'Your sins are forgiven,' and I imagine Him emphasising the word 'are'. Then He told her, 'Your faith has saved you; go in peace.' She no longer had anything to fear; her forgiveness was sealed. I am sure she immediately recognised herself in the story Jesus told, for she knew that her debt was great and she had been forgiven much. She had acknowledged her own sin and then gratefully received the forgiveness that was offered.

As it happens, I am writing this part of the book on Good Friday, and forgiveness is very much on my mind. There is so much for us to ponder during the Easter weekend, and we look forward to celebrating the glorious fulfilment of the empty tomb, which declares that the Son of Man truly was the Son of God. I absolutely rejoice in the resurrection and in the fact that I serve a living God, but I never want to gloss over the anguish, the torment and the distress that Jesus took upon Himself in order to cancel the record of debt that stood against me:

> ... cancelling the record of debt that stood against us with its legal demands. This he set aside, nailing it to the cross.
> (Colossians 2:14)

Sin creates a debt that demands to be paid, and the sacrifice of every lamb in the world was never going to be enough. The lambs could never take sin away completely; it would always continue, so those who brought the offering would never be made perfect.[23] The Father knew that our debt would only ever increase, so He drew a line, not to stop the sin, but to end the demand upon us to pay for it. Our debt was nailed to the cross, and in acknowledging this and all that it means, we can experience the full joy of the risen Saviour, because 'God made [us] alive together with him, having forgiven us all our trespasses' (Colossians 2:13).

No matter what our sin is or was, in receiving God's forgiveness, our redemption is sealed. We have nothing to fear, for we are completely forgiven. Let us not diminish what Christ has done for us by continuing to carry any past sin. Instead, let us learn to surrender it fully, leave it at the cross and live in the freedom that Jesus secured for us.

A Canaanite woman: Matthew 15:21-28

But she came and knelt before him, saying, 'Lord, help me.'
(Matthew 15:25)

In this story we find Jesus and His disciples in the coastal region of Tyre. Hearing of His arrival, a woman comes running to find Him; not a Jewish woman, but a Gentile. When she finds Him, she cries, 'Have mercy on me, O Lord, Son of David; my daughter is severely oppressed by a demon.'

The Canaanite religion had more than enough deities and we can realistically assume that this mother had prayed, or even sacrificed, to all of them. Still, her child was slipping away from her day by day, enslaved by a demon, leaving the mother distraught and running out of options. Those around her knew of her distress, and somewhere along the way she heard about Jesus. She would have known of the God of Israel because she lived in an area mixed with Jews, but

---

[23] Hebrews 10:1-4.

something had happened to make her believe that Jesus was the One who held the key to the hope that she desperately needed. Just like Bartimaeus, she addressed Him by His Messianic name.

On hearing her, Jesus did not respond, which the disciples were thinking was good and proper. How dare this Gentile woman speak to any one of the men, let alone the Rabbi! They urged Him to send her away, and He answered, 'I was sent only to the lost sheep of the house of Israel.' They nodded in approval, pleased that they did not have to deal with her. 'But she came and knelt before him, saying, "Lord, help me."' Protocol and socially acceptable behaviour faded into insignificance next to her dire situation. She had put time and energy into so many gods that neither spoke, nor moved, nor even breathed. But this man, this real, living, breathing man of miracles, the proclaimed Messiah of the Jews, now stood before her and she would not let anyone else take away her hope.

Jesus now turned and spoke to her directly, although His words did not seem kind. 'It is not right to take the children's bread and throw it to the dogs.' It feels like a harsh statement in describing the Gentiles as dogs. Was Jesus letting the disciples hear what their prejudice sounded like out loud, or was He testing the woman's resolve? As she thought of her daughter, not even humiliation deterred her as she answered, 'Yes, Lord, yet even the dogs eat the crumbs that fall from their masters' table.' Such tenacity! She was so aware of her own unworthiness that she was willing to accept the smallest fragment of bread that He might offer.

The test was over, Jesus had heard enough and He answered, 'O woman, great is your faith! Be it done for you as you desire.' She held fast to her belief and the Lord answered her plea.

This is such an amazing story of faith in the midst of hostility and prejudice. A faith that was undeterred by outside voices and opinions. A woman with a great need and a glimmer of hope came and knelt before the Lord. A crumb of mercy was all that she wanted, but she received a bounty of grace. She came, she asked, and she received in faith.

Through the most trying of circumstances, hold fast to your faith in Almighty God. His mercy and grace are immense, and although we don't even deserve the falling crumbs from His table, He has seated us beside Him at the banquet.

A royal official: John 4:46-53

Jesus said to him, 'Unless you see signs and wonders you will not believe.'
(John 4:48)

Jesus had been to the Passover feast in Jerusalem where 'many believed in his name when they saw the signs that he was doing' (John 2:23). After spending some time in the Judean countryside with His disciples, He came up through Samaria where He met the woman at Jacob's well. He stayed in that area for a couple of days before heading back to Galilee.

A royal official who lived in Capernaum had heard that Jesus had returned to Galilee. As he wanted to speak to Jesus on a personal matter, he made the journey to Cana to meet Him face to face. On meeting Jesus, the ESV says that he 'asked' Him to come and heal his son, whereas the KJV tells us he 'besought' Jesus to come. There was indeed an urgency to his request; he was imploring Jesus to accompany him back to Capernaum because his son was very close to death. Jesus answered him by saying, 'Unless you see signs and wonders you will not believe.' The truth was that a miracle was absolutely what he needed, so he asked again, 'Sir, come down before my child dies.'

Jesus had experienced no honour in His home town, and it appeared that the house of Israel only wanted Him to perform, yet the Gentiles simply accepted His words. Jesus was here, however, to do the will of the Father, and right now He had an earthly father in front of Him who loved his own son dearly and did not want him to die. Jesus honoured the request of the official, and said, 'Go; your son will live.' Before reaching home, some of his servants came to meet him on the road with the good news that his son was recovering. So, curious about the timing, he asked at what precise hour his son began to show signs of recovery. The servants replied, 'Yesterday at the seventh hour the fever left him.' We read, 'The father knew that was the hour when Jesus had said to him, "Your son will live." And he himself believed, and all his household.'

The official went looking for a miracle worker and ended up finding the Messiah. He may not have recognised this truth immediately, but when the realisation dawned, faith took hold. He had wanted Jesus to come and perform, but Jesus told him to go and believe. In trusting the word of Jesus, his life changed, along with those of his entire household.

The Lord may not always do things the way we want Him to, but He *will* always work for our good; all we have to do is trust His direction.

Faithful in faith

Faith comes in various ways and each of us will have a unique encounter with Jesus. The similarity for us is that it always begins with a response to His call of, 'Follow Me.' Faith is our choice but it is His path, and the cost to us comes nowhere close to the price that He paid for our salvation. Faith requires commitment and it is most definitely a continual process, but when we entrust our lives wholly to God, we entrust them to the One who can keep our feet from falling, so that we can walk before Him 'in the light of life' (Psalm 56:13). The path may be narrow and there will undoubtedly be obstacles along the way, but the One we follow is 'guarding the paths of justice and watching over the way of his saints' (Proverbs 2:8).

The Lord is faithful in guarding and guiding our steps as we follow Him. In return, we must be faithful in both our walk and our work, for our faith needs to be worked out in practical ways. When Jesus called Simon, Andrew, James and John, He said to them, 'Follow me, and I will make you fishers of men' (Matthew 4:19). He didn't say, 'Follow Me, sit back and relax.' Far from it, because we can't follow by remaining where we are. Following is an active response. There is kingdom work to be done here and now and the Lord has a job for each one of us to do. We are servants of the King, working for His pleasure and glory. Each of us has a personalised role, for which the bonuses and benefits are out of this world.

Reflections

Questions

- As you think about how the centurion exercised faith, what are the circumstances that you bring to Jesus and what are the ones you don't? Why is there a difference?

- Jesus spoke directly to Bartimaeus and asked, 'What do you want me to do for you?' Imagine Him asking you the same question. What would your answer be?

- Do you struggle at times to accept that you have been completely forgiven? Why is your answer 'yes' or why is it 'no'?

Practical application

Think about any past sin that you are holding on to and write it down on a piece of paper. Hold it in your hand and acknowledge before God that it has been paid for by the blood of Jesus on the cross. Now rip it up and throw it away, confidently believing that you have been completely forgiven.

Prayer

Thank You, Lord Jesus, for taking all of my sin to the cross. I know that I have been forgiven, that my redemption has been sealed and I can walk in the truth of my salvation. Help me, Lord, to never diminish what You have done for me by continuing to carry any past sin. Help me to surrender it fully and to leave it at the cross, so that I can live in the freedom that You secured for me. Amen.

6

Teachings on the kingdom

*What is the kingdom of God like? And to what shall I
compare it?*
(Luke 13:18)

Before delving into this chapter, take a moment to envisage
the kingdom of God. The question I have for you is, 'Where
is it?'

In Mark 12, we hear Jesus having a conversation with a
scribe who had asked Him which commandment is the
greatest. Jesus responded, telling him that it is to love the
Lord your God with all your heart, soul, mind and strength,
and then to 'love your neighbour as yourself' (v31). The
scribe complimented Jesus on giving the right answer and
then proceeded to expound the Scriptures by affirming that
to love God with your whole being and to love your
neighbour is much more than burnt offerings and sacrifices.
This particular scribe appears to have understood God's
heart better than the majority of his peers, and Jesus,
acknowledging his wisdom, said to him, 'You are not far from
the kingdom of God' (v34).

Physically speaking, this scribe was within touching
distance of the kingdom of God, but Jesus was talking
spiritually, and spiritually speaking, he was also within
touching distance of the kingdom of God.

Part of Jesus' purpose on earth was to explain the truth of the kingdom, and as the Son of God, He was bringing the kingdom of God closer than ever before. This was (and is) important because it is not only the residence of the King of kings, but it is also the eternal home for every child of God. Even for the seasoned Christian, the whole concept of a tangible, vibrant, glorious, pure and perfect place in the heavens above the heavens is mind-blowing.[24] Add to that the truth that part of God's kingdom lives within every one of us who has accepted Jesus as Saviour and Lord, and well, 'wow' just seems incredibly insufficient! Seeing the kingdom as not only in the heavens but also here on earth, how, then, do these two opposing worlds live side by side?

If you did the exercise at the start of the chapter, you will know how complex it can be to think about the kingdom of God. So how do we start to explain it? Imagine, if you will, having the task of explaining the colour green to someone who has been blind from birth. In Ireland, we have forty shades of that one colour, so how do you even begin to describe the whole spectrum of the rainbow? How do you convey what is unfathomable?

Jesus had the amazing ability to portray heavenly truth to earthly minds, and in Matthew 13, He spent time explaining the kingdom in ways and concepts that were relatable to all those listening to Him. We are going to take a look at some of the parables that He used to help us understand this complex and intriguing phenomenon. The five we will be looking at are the parables of the weeds, the mustard seed, the leaven, the hidden treasure and the pearl. You might find it helpful to have a Bible with you as we look at each parable in turn, or you may want to take a few minutes now to read through them first of all.

---

[24] Revelation 7; 21.

The parable of the weeds: Matthew 13:24-30, 36-43

For those of you who are gardeners, weeds are most certainly the bane of your garden. If a weed is growing next to a plant, it is so difficult to kill the one without harming the other. The roots of a weed can be so strong that it can be almost impossible to pull them out. Jesus brought this parable and said to His listeners:

> The kingdom of heaven may be compared to a man who sowed good seed in his field, but while his men were sleeping, his enemy came and sowed weeds among the wheat and went away.
> (Matthew 13:24-25)

In this story, when the servants came to tell the master about the state of the field, they were told to leave the weeds where they were, 'lest in gathering the weeds you root up the wheat along with them. Let both grow together until the harvest.'

Jesus explained that the field represents the world, He is the sower and 'the good seed is the sons of the kingdom'. The enemy is the devil, who sows evil in the darkness; the good and the evil then inevitably grow side by side. This is the world in which we live, where the children of light and the children of darkness cohabit; two different species existing in the same space.

The reality of this living arrangement means that we are forced to see humanity's inhumanity on a daily basis, and it is nothing short of devastating. The question is often asked as to why God doesn't intervene in certain circumstances and why evil is allowed to persist. God's purpose and reasoning are things that we can never fully grasp, but this truth remains – God wants to redeem those who practise evil in exactly the same way that He wants to redeem those who practise good, 'for all have sinned and fall short of the glory of God'

(Romans 3:23). Don't misunderstand this as acceptance of horrific evil, and that God is not disturbed by it.

Let me take you back into the Old Testament for just a moment to have a glimpse at how God feels about the atrocities we see all around His world:

> The LORD saw that the wickedness of man was great in the earth, and that every intention of the thoughts of his heart was only evil continually. And the LORD was sorry that he had made man on the earth, and it grieved him to his heart. So the LORD said, 'I will blot out man whom I have created from the face of the land, man and animals and creeping things and birds of the heavens, for I am sorry that I have made them.'
> (Genesis 6:5-7)

God didn't blot mankind out entirely because Noah had found favour in His eyes (v8). On God's instruction, Noah built a floating home, within which he and his family, along with breeding pairs of every animal, were saved from the coming destruction of the flood. From Adam to the flood was just under 1,700 years, and God's creation 'grieved him to his heart'. Move forward another 1,700 years and the extent of God's grief is once again evident:

> 'I will utterly sweep away everything
> from the face of the earth,' declares the LORD.
> 'I will sweep away man and beast;
> I will sweep away the birds of the heavens
> and the fish of the sea,
> and the rubble with the wicked.
> I will cut off mankind
> from the face of the earth,' declares the LORD …
> 'For my decision is to gather nations,
> to assemble kingdoms,
> to pour out upon them my indignation,
> all my burning anger;

for in the fire of my jealousy
all the earth shall be consumed.'
(Zephaniah 1:2-3; 3:8)

God is not oblivious to evil; He sees it all too well, but He
made a promise, saying, 'I will never again curse the ground
because of man ... Neither will I ever again strike down every
living creature as I have done' (Genesis 8:21). To this day,
God's sorrow is great because of the evil that lives within His
creation, and the verses in Zephaniah tell us that judgement
is coming. However, where there is judgement, there is
mercy.

People often find it hard to reconcile the God of the Old
Testament with the God of the New Testament. The former
appears harsh, vengeful and violent, while the latter is filled
with love, grace and hope. Careful examination of Scripture
reveals God's consistency and the truth about His apparent
contradictory nature. In fact, when we look at any of the
prophetic books, they are condensed versions of the whole
Bible. Each book declares God's judgement while offering
the hand of mercy; each book presents a choice. That is the
arc of the Bible – justice and mercy. The Old Testament
highlights God's justice which was birthed from sorrow, and
the New Testament highlights His mercy, which was birthed
from love:

> For to us a child is born,
> to us a son is given.
> (Isaiah 9:6)

> God did not send his Son into the world to condemn
> the world, but in order that the world might be saved
> through him.
> (John 3:17)

Jesus is the mercy that has been sent down and given to the
world, and through the parable of the weeds He addresses

the issue that judgement has its allotted time: 'at harvest time I will tell the reapers, Gather the weeds first and bind them in bundles to be burned, but gather the wheat into my barn.' The harvest represents 'the close of the age', the end of time. During this final harvest of all time, the angels 'will gather out of his kingdom all causes of sin and all law-breakers, and throw them into the fiery furnace'. This is God's judgement in God's time.

For now, the wheat and the weeds live side by side until the appointed time that God has chosen. This will be a glorious day for every follower of Jesus; a day when 'the righteous will shine like the sun in the kingdom of their Father'.

The parable of the mustard seed: Matthew 13:31-32

The Palestine mustard plant was widely grown and was something that people would have planted in their own pots, courtyard or field, so that is where Jesus starts with this parable:

> The kingdom of heaven is like a grain of mustard seed that a man took and sowed in his field. It is the smallest of all seeds, but when it has grown it is larger than all the garden plants and becomes a tree, so that the birds of the air come and make nests in its branches.
> (Matthew 13:31-32)

No explanation of this parable has been recorded in the Gospels, so what is Jesus telling us through the mustard seed? The image He portrays of the tree is something strong and beautiful, as well as being of great necessity.

The followers of Jesus were small in number at first, but from twelve apostles the Church would grow. It would expand across countries and continents, and the lost, the lonely, the outcast and the vulnerable would all find safety and shelter within it, for the 'birds of the air come and make nests in its branches'. The 'birds of the air' is a collective term for every species, depicting every nation, tribe and tongue being able to find a home in the Church of God. The book of Revelation confirms this wonderful truth of salvation for all, for it says, 'a great multitude that no one could number, from every nation, from all tribes and peoples and languages, [were] standing before the throne and before the Lamb, clothed in white robes, with palm branches in their hands' (Revelation 7:9). What a testimony to the mustard seed!

The mustard seed may be tiny but its power is immense, which we also saw earlier when Jesus used this same seed to create an image of our faith. This seed represents quality, substance and power. Every son and daughter of the kingdom has this power within them, and collectively they (we) are part of something strong and beautiful, and of great necessity. We are part of the universal Church of God.

The parable of the leaven: Matthew 13:33

Bread was such a major part of the daily diet that it was present at every meal. Every home would have a measure of leaven, or yeast, which would be added to dough, then covered and put away. It would get to work immediately, spreading through the mixture to change its volume and flavour. In explaining the kingdom, this short, one-sentence parable gets straight to the point: 'The kingdom of heaven is like leaven that a woman took and hid in three measures of flour, till it was all leavened.'

When leavened flour was used to create a dough, the change it made on the inside became evident on the outside, enhancing it from its original state and enabling it to spread. The message here is that as sons and daughters of the kingdom with the power of God within us, we can have a positive influence on those around us. As we allow God to work through us in this way, we will witness His Church grow and expand.

On the flip side of that, we need to be wary, because not all influence is good. It could be, and indeed it should be, but unfortunately that's not always the case. Jesus wanted His followers to be wary 'of the leaven of the Pharisees, which is hypocrisy' (Luke 12:1).

The Pharisees had a responsibility to the people, but as leaders they had wandered far from the path, becoming absorbed in the power of their position rather than the power of El Shaddai, the Almighty God. These were holy men who taught the law but didn't always practise it themselves, which meant that their influence caused more harm to the Jews than good.

We need to pray that our influence is always for the good; a positive influence that encourages a positive change in the lives of those we come into contact with, drawing them into the kingdom of God.

The parables of the hidden treasure and the pearl: Matthew 13:44-46

Those listening to Jesus had grown up with the words of the Hebrew Bible, hearing them in the synagogue as well as the home. They knew the stories of their forefathers Abraham, Isaac and Jacob, but probably felt very far removed from the God of that time; a somewhat unobtainable and unseen God.

Now, the unobtainable was a tangible presence right in front of them, and yet it almost feels like Jesus was hidden in plain sight. All they had to do was open their eyes, but they appeared unable to do so: 'This is why I speak to them in parables, because seeing they do not see, and hearing they do not hear, nor do they understand' (Matthew 13:13). So Jesus asked them to use their imaginations and to visualise a man who comes across a treasure hidden in a field and, immediately recognising its worth, 'goes and sells all that he has and buys that field'.

Not wanting them to get caught up in the quantity of the treasure, Jesus asked them to imagine a merchant who searches out only the finest of pearls. In his search he comes across a single pearl, whose worth seems to have eluded everyone else who has seen it. In understanding its value, he 'went and sold all that he had and bought it'.

Through both of these parables, Jesus pointed out three things: 1) There is a treasure to be found. 2) The treasure has a cost. 3) The treasure has a value which completely eclipses the cost. I wonder how many people that day could see the treasure standing before them?

This incredible treasure that we find in Christ is beyond comparison to anything else on earth, but how willing are we to give up everything for Him? Maybe the word 'everything' is sounding a bit extreme, but think about it in the context of the person who is still searching for Christ. In the two scenarios that Jesus shared, the person who discovers the amazing treasure is willing to give up everything they have in pursuit of something even better. The old life is no longer important because the promise of the new life is much more precious.

In Chapter Four we looked at what Jesus said regarding the cost of following Him in terms of everyday challenges, outside circumstances and the attitude of others. If we were now to think about it in terms of our own personal pursuits, what are we willing to give up in order to enjoy Him more? If Jesus is our treasure, is it enough to only gaze on Him once a week? That doesn't seem right, does it? If we had sold everything we owned in order to purchase this treasure, there would be no way we would let it out of our sight for any length of time. If it was the only thing we owned, this valuable find would be carried with us everywhere, for we would want to look at it always.

Jesus is the most valuable thing we will ever have in our possession. He is like the diamond in the display case that doesn't have a price tag, for His worth is incalculable. He is the one thing that we need in our lives above everything else. Jesus sees *our* true worth; the question is, are we seeing His? To be willing to give up what is temporary in order to gain what is eternal is the essence of true kingdom discipleship.

As kingdom disciples, Jesus has helped us to see how influential we can be individually, and how productive we can be collectively. He has shown us who we are in the kingdom and the reality of what we will contend with in the world around us. He has also shown us that we have great strength when we work together as the family of God in showing compassion and kindness to those far and near. Without a doubt, the greatest thing we could ever do is help others find the greatest treasure on earth.

In following Jesus, we follow His example, and as He worked for the glory of the kingdom, so must we.

Kingdom workers

In Matthew 19 we read the story of a rich young man in search of eternal life. He asked Jesus what he should do to receive this life, and Jesus directed him to the commandments. The young man confirmed that he was already doing this, so what more could he do? Jesus said, 'If you would be perfect, go, sell what you possess and give to the poor, and you will have treasure in heaven; and come, follow me' (v21). This was a step too far for the young man, because he had great wealth.

Simon Peter then turned to Jesus with a question of his own: 'See, we have left everything and followed you. What then will we have?' (v27).

Was Peter looking for some kind of earthly reward for giving everything up to follow Jesus, or did he perhaps feel deserving of some sort of recognition? Whatever his reason was for asking the question, the answer he received must have blown him away. 'Truly, I say to you, in the new world, when the Son of Man will sit on his glorious throne, you who have followed me will also sit on twelve thrones, judging the twelve tribes of Israel' (v28). I am sure that kept Peter quiet for a moment or two as he digested the thought, and the honour within it.

The question that Peter asked, however, reflects the heart of people everywhere. When asked to help with something, the reply (or internal thought) can be, 'What's in it for me?' Jesus put forward another parable that challenges the notion of 'deserved recognition'.

Labourers in the vineyard: Matthew 20:1-16

For the kingdom of heaven is like a master of a house who went out early in the morning to hire labourers for his vineyard. After agreeing with the labourers for a denarius a day, he sent them into his vineyard. And going out about the third hour he saw others standing idle in the market-place, and to them he said, 'You go into the vineyard too, and whatever is right I will give you.' So they went. Going out again about the sixth hour and the ninth hour, he did the same. And about the eleventh hour he went out and found others standing. And he said to them, 'Why do you stand here idle all day?' They said to him, 'Because no one has hired us.' He said to them, 'You go into the vineyard too.' And when evening came, the owner of the vineyard said to his foreman, 'Call the labourers and pay them their wages, beginning with the last, up to the first.' And when those hired about the eleventh hour came, each of them received a denarius. Now when those hired first came, they thought they would receive more, but each of them also received a denarius. And on receiving it they grumbled at the master of the house, saying, 'These last worked only one hour, and you have made them equal to us who have borne the burden of the day and the scorching heat.' But he replied to one of them, 'Friend, I am doing you no wrong. Did you not agree with me for a denarius? Take what belongs to you and go. I choose to give to this last worker as I give to you. Am I not allowed to do what I choose with what belongs to me? Or do you begrudge my generosity?' So the last will be first, and the first last.

What do you hear Jesus saying through this parable? What thoughts or images come to your mind? Is it the idea of inequality among Christians? Is it deathbed salvation? Is it simply people at different stages of life finding Jesus and entering the kingdom workforce? Or, perhaps, recognition for what we do for God? Whatever your initial thoughts may be, this truly is a very poignant parable.

In this story, people join the workforce at different times throughout the day. At the end of the working day, the foreman attends to the wages, with everyone receiving the same pay. This does not go down well with those who started first thing in morning, and we are told that 'they grumbled at the master of the house' (v11). The workers who started at 6am felt that they deserved more for their labour than those who came much later, so the master asks them, 'Do you begrudge my generosity?' (v15). Wow, what a question! How often do we grumble at God and question what is fair? How often do we look at what others have and wonder why our blessing doesn't seem as generous?

Although in this parable Jesus is challenging our attitude towards our service (which is something that will be explored in the next chapter) and how we view the service of others, its main focus is on the attitude and behaviour of the master of the vineyard. Just as he went out continually to look for workers, God the Father never stops looking for those to bring into the kingdom, and He will keep searching up until the final hour. Everyone who responds to His call will each receive the same salvation.

Our God is a generous God, so whether a person has served Him for decades or, like the thief on the cross, has only moments to praise Him, the reward remains the same, eternal life in His kingdom: 'Come, you who are blessed by my Father, inherit the kingdom prepared for you from the foundation of the world' (Matthew 25:34).

This is the blessing above all blessings, to have, as an inheritance, the kingdom of our God, shared in equal measure with all the sons and daughters of the King. The inheritance that God gives His children, He has been preparing from before the beginning of creation. Isn't that incredible? He knew what He wanted to give to us from the very start of time, and He does it with joy: 'it is your Father's good pleasure to give you the kingdom' (Luke 12:32).

As 'heirs with Christ' (Romans 8:17), every blessing we have comes through Him. The Father looks on us as He looks on the Son and grants us an unrestrained bounty of favour. He holds nothing back from us, so we should hold nothing back from Him as we serve in His vineyard.

Reflections

Questions

- As you read about the wheat and the weeds, in what ways are you better able to understand God's judgement and God's mercy, regarding the world that we live in?

- Jesus wants us to have a positive influence on those around us. What do you think that would look like in your everyday life?

- Are there things that you have found hard to give up, or is there something that you know you should give up but are struggling to let go of? Is there anyone you can speak to about this, a trusted Christian friend or leader?

Practical application

Choose something that you know takes up too much of your time – it might be social media, games on your phone, endless videos of animals doing daft things, etc – and limit yourself on this activity for one week. Whatever amount of time was usually spent, reduce it by half and spend the other half reading the Gospel of Matthew. Review what has happened in your faith journey after the week.

Prayer

Father God, please show me the things in my life that are distracting me from spending time with You. Help me to fully understand that what I have in You always outweighs anything that this world offers. I pray that those around me would see a positive change in my life and that I would be a good influence in the lives of others, so that they too would be drawn to You. In Jesus' name. Amen.

7

Teaching the right attitude

By this all people will know that you are my disciples,
if you have love for one another.
(John 13:35)

It may sound strange, or maybe surprising, that having the right attitude starts from a place of genuine love. True love is a powerful thing, and it is most visible through our behaviour and our attitude. When we come to faith in Christ there is a shift in how we look at the world. Our perspective changes, what drives us changes and our attitude changes. A kind of realignment takes place in our heart and mind and some of the things (or maybe a lot of the things) that we once did no longer feel right. Rufus McDaniel summed it up well when he penned these words:

> What a wonderful change in my life has been wrought
> Since Jesus came into my heart!
> I have light in my soul for which long I had sought,
> Since Jesus came into my heart![25]

The change that takes place within us causes us to look *at* things differently and to look *for* things differently. The things

---

[25] Rufus Henry McDaniel (1850-1940), 'Since Jesus Came into My Heart'. Public domain.

around us in the world can no longer satisfy the soul as they once did, and it is only the pure things of God, displayed through Christ Jesus, that bring us fulfilment.

The Holy Spirit guides us as we seek out the pure things of God, and then helps us to grow in them, changing our priorities, our attitudes and behaviours from the inside. Through the Spirit, we develop a deeper understanding of (and the need for) kindness, gentleness, patience, goodness, humility, forgiveness, respect, empathy, love: heavenly attributes in an earthly life.

Seeking these things takes conscious effort because they don't come to us naturally, as God had intended. Our physical state (often referred to in the Bible as 'the flesh'[26]) will always be a hindrance to our spiritual state, which is why we have to actively pursue these godly attributes. Everything we do is an expression of who we are, for better or for worse. Our actions, our attitudes and our words all tell the story of who we are. Does that story contain genuine love? For the Christian, there is an obligation to demonstrate love in our everyday lives. There is no excuse for it not to be there and there is no excuse for not knowing 'how'.

God showed us how:

> But God shows his love for us in that while we were still sinners, Christ died for us.
> (Romans 5:8)

Jesus showed us how:

> Just as I have loved you, you also are to love one another. By this all people will know that you are my disciples.
> (John 13:34-35)

---

[26] See, for example, Romans 8:2-13.

As well as showing us how to love by way of His personal actions, Jesus showed us through the lessons that He taught. Fundamentally, our behaviour towards others, in all circumstances, begins with a basic rule; a golden rule, which states, 'So whatever you wish that others would do to you, do also to them' (Matthew 7:12).

That sounds easy enough, doesn't it? You respect me, I respect you; you show kindness to me and I'll show kindness to you. Not exactly. In fact, that is not at all what this verse is saying. This is not a tit-for-tat niceness scale; we are not repaying in kind the actions of another. This is about treating people in the correct manner, regardless of their actions. How we act is proactive, not reactive.

How do you wish to be treated? My list includes respect, honesty and consideration.

An attitude of forgiveness

The golden rule goes hand in hand with the second great commandment, to love our neighbour as ourselves. The level of ease or difficulty in expressing genuine love depends (for us) on the recipient. How do we treat someone with respect and consideration when they have caused us untold pain and all we feel is anger and contempt? The direction from Jesus is simple and clear: 'forgive, if you have anything against anyone, so that your Father also who is in heaven may forgive you your trespasses' (Mark 11:25). OK, maybe not simple, but definitely clear.

In everyday life, forgiveness may prove to be the most difficult attitude and behaviour to master, and I say this from personal experience. When I gave my life to Jesus, I knew that I had been forgiven. The forgiveness I had received covered every bad thing I had ever done and every bad thought I had ever had, regardless of whether I could remember them or even appreciate what they were. I had also been forgiven for the good things that I should have done but failed to do. Forgiveness was the cornerstone of my salvation.

As time went on and I studied God's Word, I became more aware of all the things that displeased God and were sinful in His eyes, and my prayers for forgiveness became more detailed. To come before God in true repentance is sometimes an emotional experience, but it is always followed by a calmness and peace. I can feel this beautiful peace of God because of His mercy and grace, which He freely gives to every repentant heart. In being honest about my sin and obedient to His Word, I experience the freedom that forgiveness brings.

This wonderful feeling of being forgiven carried me along for some time, but then difficult experiences took place, causing hurt and pain to take root. Now the shoe was on the other foot and I found that I couldn't forgive the wrong that had been done to me. I still approached the throne of grace with the same expectancy of God's forgiveness to me, but the peace didn't always follow. I would say the Lord's Prayer in church along with everyone else, but when it came to, 'And forgive us our trespasses, as we forgive those who trespass against us',[27] I could barely get the words out past the lump in my throat.

Unforgiveness has such a debilitating force, spiritually, physically and mentally. In the middle of my struggle, there was a constant gentle voice telling me that I needed to forgive, I needed to hand it over and let go because the only person being hurt by my unforgiveness was me. Withheld forgiveness is the devil's snare. But forgiveness is hard when there is no apology or no request to be forgiven; there is no sign of repentance. God requires repentance, so why shouldn't I?

It doesn't work like that, though. I am seeking a deep personal relationship with God and I don't want any

[27] www.churchofengland.org/faith-calling/what-we-believe/lords-prayer (accessed 15th April 2024). See Matthew 6:12.

obstacles to be in the way of that. Jesus tells me, 'For if you forgive others their trespasses, your heavenly Father will also forgive you' (Matthew 6:14). I need His forgiveness, and that need is so much greater than my need to withhold forgiveness from someone else.

The lesson in this is not to let the devil trap us in a maze of pain, hurt and resentment but to fully trust in the restoring power of Jesus to bring healing, wholeness and peace back to our life. He knows that we will encounter hurt and distress, but He doesn't want us to carry that kind of burden, which is why He carried it to the cross. The cross brings freedom through forgiveness. We experience this freedom through the mercy and grace that God affords us, and we also experience it through the mercy and grace we give to others.

If an attitude of forgiveness is something that you personally struggle with, I would encourage you to seek God's direction, asking Him to guide you in making this practice a reality in your life, so that you can truly live free.

Non-judgemental behaviour

Seeking the Father's help is a continuous process as we learn how to treat everyone with the same grace, compassion and love that God has shown to us. These characteristics are lost when we become judge and jury of other people's behaviour. Jesus directs us in this, saying, 'Judge not, and you will not be judged; condemn not, and you will not be condemned' (Luke 6:37).

The issue with human judgement is that it is not consistent; what I find offensive in someone you might find acceptable, and vice versa. When we judge others (let's not pretend we don't), it comes from our own personal set of values. We each have a standard that we deem to be respectable, adequate and tolerable in others. When those standards are breached, we feel justified in passing judgement. That is where the problem starts because there is an immeasurable difference between God's holy standards and our self-righteous standards.

Jesus highlights the problem in judging by asking, 'Why do you see the speck that is in your brother's eye, but do not notice the log that is in your own eye?' (Matthew 7:3). How quickly we can make excuses to justify our own actions and yet feel vindicated in pointing to the flaw in the actions of someone else! This kind of hypocritical behaviour has severe consequences: 'For with the judgment you pronounce you will be judged, and with the measure you use it will be measured to you' (Matthew 7:2).

This should cause all of us to pause and think carefully before we throw that first stone.[28] People will always do things that we don't like, and things that we don't understand, but before we start talking *about* them, perhaps we should talk *to* them. We are all flawed people, and flawed people do not always do the right thing. Just to be clear, Jesus does not want us to excuse or ignore wrong behaviour; after all, it is in acknowledging it that we receive forgiveness. The key, Jesus says, to addressing it in someone else is to do it from a clear perspective – 'first take the log out of your own eye, and then you will see clearly to take the speck out of your brother's eye' (Matthew 7:5).

If we don't do it this way, then it becomes the blind leading the blind, and what happens then? 'Will they not both fall into a pit?' (Luke 6:39). A clear perspective and prayerful consideration enable us to talk to someone about a situation in an understanding way and lead them by the truth of God's Word back onto the right path.

Changing behaviour

Part of the behaviour realignment process is a change of viewpoint. It is not always easy to change a particular behaviour, especially if it is something that has been done in

---

[28] John 8:7.

the same way for a long time. Have you ever found yourself caught in a loop of doing the same thing over and over, regardless of the results, because that is what worked in the past? Are you holding on to old routines and practices that are failing to produce the outcome that you want? Have you considered that somewhere in your peripheral vision God is trying to get your attention?

Let's consider, for example, the primary school teacher with little ones who are hyperactive, easily distracted or just little chatterboxes. Every morning it is the same struggle just to get the roll call completed. This should be an easy task but it has become exhausting; something needs to change. 'Lord, I need help.' Then they remember a suggestion from a friend that they had previously ignored, on the grounds that it sounded daft, but realistically, what is there to lose? Now all the kids have a 'role' to play as they stand in a circle and 'call' out the name of the person next to them. Around they go, one by one, until the circle is complete. It turns out that the kids love this routine and can't wait to play every morning. Happy children, happy teacher.

Four of the disciples – Simon, Andrew, James and John – were all seasoned fishermen and knew exactly how to fish, where to fish and when to fish. One particular night, they went out in what were probably good conditions and with the correct equipment. They adopted their usual routine and waited. The nets were hauled in; nothing, and so began the loop. Throw nets out, wait, haul nets in, nothing. Throw nets out, wait, haul nets in, nothing. It's bearable the first few times, but as the hours pass, despair and frustration grow. As dawn breaks, it's time to admit defeat, but then a voice speaks:

> Jesus said to them, 'Children, do you have any fish?' They answered him, 'No.' He said to them, 'Cast the net on the right side of the boat, and you will find

some.' So they cast it, and now they were not able to haul it in, because of the quantity of fish.
(John 21:5-6)

They could have ignored the advice and let the situation end in failure, but the person on the shore had got their attention, and their willingness to change behaviour brought about a change in circumstances.

If we are caught in a loop of frustration, monotony or exhaustion, it's probably time to stop and listen for the voice with advice. Frustrating routines don't necessarily mean we are on the wrong path (or in the wrong boat); we may just need a change of tactics. If the long commute to work is getting more stressful, maybe it time to take the co-worker up on their car-share offer, or maybe even try the train once a week. Just because we have done something the same way for as long as we can remember, we should never be afraid to allow the Lord to show us a different way.

Changing routines and practices isn't easy and we won't always get it right first time, but having the openness to listen and the courage to address the issues is a good first step. It is so easy for us to get caught up in the rituals of how things have always been done, and maybe nowhere more so than in church itself.

Going to church on Sunday becomes, for some, just something that is the thing to be seen doing, but this is what angered Jesus so much about the Pharisees and scribes. Their religious activity was all for show and their holier-than-thou talk was pure lip service. Their hypocritical nature seemed to know no bounds, and Jesus called them out on it. He could see through the bluster straight into their hearts, which revealed that God's ways were practically out of view:

For the sake of your tradition you have made void the word of God ...
'This people honours me with their lips,
but their heart is far from me;

100

in vain do they worship me,
teaching as doctrines the commandments of men.'
(Matthew 15:6, 8-9)

Unfortunately, hypocrisy is not exclusive to Pharisees, and lip service is still alive and well in God's Church. We sit, we listen, we get up and say, 'That was a great service,' and then we go on with our week without allowing that 'great word' to change us in any way. I wish I could say that I wasn't guilty of this, and I also wish that I could say that I have never worshipped God in vain. To praise and worship God through music and song has always been a big part of my life, but there are times when the flesh takes over from the spirit. My heart desires to sing but my mind is more concerned about the speed of the song, the tempo being wrong or the drums being too loud, and I lose the reason for singing. This is so far removed from true worship. Jesus said that 'the true worshippers will worship the Father in spirit and truth, for the Father is seeking such people to worship him' (John 4:23). When our attitude in worship is not where it should be, it affects our union with the Spirit. Yet God in His grace waits for us patiently; He waits for us to come and say, 'I am sorry, Lord.' Don't be afraid to ask for His help, for it is only in acknowledging our weaknesses and our shortcomings that we can benefit from His strength. He wants to strengthen each one of us, 'so that the name of our Lord Jesus may be glorified in you, and you in him, according to the grace of our God and the Lord Jesus Christ' (2 Thessalonians 1:12).

The Pharisees may have been guilty of lip service, but there were also those who fell into the trap of eye service, also known as people-pleasing: 'for they loved the glory that comes from man more than the glory that comes from God' (John 12:43). Are we always striving for the glory that comes from God? If not, why not?

The need to please, or to be seen doing things that please, can come from a fear of not fitting in, or the fear of being excluded. Mostly, it comes down to the basic need to be accepted:

> Nevertheless, many even of the authorities believed in him [Jesus], but for fear of the Pharisees they did not confess it, so that they would not be put out of the synagogue.
> (John 12:42)

These leaders prioritised other people above God; their focus was horizontal instead of vertical. If God is taking second place in our life, then He is not God of our life. The glory that comes from friends and peers is short-lived, and like everything else in this world, it eventually fades away. Status and position mean nothing to God, and they should not be influencing our attitude or behaviour. The only place we need to fear being excluded from is the kingdom of heaven. Everything we do and say should be for God's glory, and His alone.

A heavenly attitude

When Jesus gave His sermon on the mountain in Matthew 5–7, His message was all about attitude and behaviour. He talked about being peacemakers, showing mercy, being salt on the earth and light in the world. He talked about the dangers of anger and lust, hate and retaliation. He addressed anxieties and concerns, fasting and praying, giving, receiving and storing things up:

> Do not lay up for yourselves treasures on earth, where moth and rust destroy and where thieves break in and steal.
> (Matthew 6:19)

If you watch television at all, you will be aware that we appear to be a nation of hoarders. Jesus pointed out the dangers of accumulating what we do not need, and that material possessions will eventually rot away. His advice was not to put our energy into stockpiling earthly goods and storing up greedily for personal satisfaction. He knew that the dark part of us is never satisfied – the passions of our flesh, the desires of the body and the mind[29] – for it will always crave more. He reminds us to 'Take care, and be on your guard against all covetousness, for one's life does not consist in the abundance of one's possessions' (Luke 12:15). What a sobering verse. Instead, we are to invest our time and energy in the things of God and the extension of His kingdom. Things like kindness, compassion, goodness and generosity towards others:

> But lay up for yourselves treasures in heaven ... For where your treasure is, there your heart will be also.
> (Matthew 6:20-21)

Although kindness, compassion and generosity are all outward expressions, they are to be done in humility. Jesus is very clear when He says, 'Beware of practising your righteousness before other people ... when you give to the needy, sound no trumpet' (Matthew 6:1-2). There is no showboating in the kingdom of God. We can either get praise from people or give glory to God, but we can't do both.

When Jesus gave this message, there were those who thought that they *could* do both, and their ostentatious behaviour was always on display in their giving, their praying and their fasting. Jesus had no time for hypocrisy, and He had no problem pointing out this religious act of false humility and righteousness.

In Matthew 6:2, it is interesting to note that Jesus did not say 'if' you give but 'when' you give; this is something we are clearly expected to do. The emphasis, though, is not on how much we give but on how we give it, which should be quietly and without drawing attention. What we give is between us

---

[29] Ephesians 2:3.

and the Lord, and the only recognition worth anything comes from, 'your Father who sees in secret [and] will reward you' (Matthew 6:4).

An attitude of giving

The father-heart of God aches for the neglected, and He directs His people in this regard with a clear instruction, 'You shall open wide your hand to your brother, to the needy and to the poor, in your land' (Deuteronomy 15:11). The Lord wants us to be kind, considerate and compassionate people; people who reflect His standards and live according to His ways. For the Pharisees (who did nothing quietly, but preferred to draw attention to everything), giving was all about the tithe, which they had practically turned into an art form. Jesus could not stand their double standards, and pointed out this truth: 'you tithe mint and dill and cumin, and have neglected the weightier matters of the law: justice and mercy and faithfulness' (Matthew 23:23). They had forgotten the true essence of what it meant to give as an act of worship to God. We too can get so entangled in the ritual of Christianity that we lose sight of what God truly requires of us.

Jesus used the subject of giving to illustrate what a true heart of worship looks like. He was sitting on the steps between the temple courtyard and the court of the women, opposite the treasury, and had observed people putting money into the offering box. Jesus had watched the rich put in large sums, but His attention was drawn when 'a poor widow came and put in two small copper coins, which make a penny' (Mark 12:42). Calling His disciples, He said to them:

> Truly, I say to you, this poor widow has put in more than all those who are contributing to the offering box. For they all contributed out of their abundance,

but she out of her poverty has put in everything she
had, all she had to live on.
(Mark 12:43-44)

The widow gave two copper coins, two *lepta*, the smallest unit
of money available (imagine the old sterling halfpenny). So
this is not a lesson in tithing, for how do you tithe a penny?
This is about giving all that you have. This lady gave out of
her poverty, or, as the KJV says, 'but she of her want did cast
in all'. She was among those that we would class as being in
need. She was among those towards whom God has said to
'open wide your hand' (Deuteronomy 15:11). Other people
in a similar position to her would be found at the gate of the
temple begging for alms. So what was it about her that caused
her to give up what she needed most?

In coming to the temple and handing over all that she had,
this poor widow was demonstrating her faith in Jehovah Jireh
– the God who provides. She may even have heard Jesus say,
'Do not be anxious, saying, "What shall we eat?" or "What
shall we drink?" or "What shall we wear?" … your heavenly
Father knows that you need them all' (Matthew 6:31-32),
which may have strengthened her faith even more. Just like
the parable in Matthew 13 of the man who found the
treasure, sold all that he had and bought the field, I believe
this widow had found something so valuable that everything
else paled in comparison.

You may have already worked out that this lesson goes
way beyond money; it is a lesson in giving all of yourself to
God – your family, your home, your work, your relationships,
your decisions. When we give everything over to the Lord's
keeping, we will never be poorer for it. In fact, we will be
richer in ways we never thought possible. This is because
when we have a clearer understanding of what God requires
of us, we can give Him what He deserves *from* us:

He has told you, O man, what is good;
and what does the LORD require of you

105

but to do justice, and to love kindness,
and to walk humbly with your God?
(Micah 6:8)

God requires a Christlike attitude and visible change of behaviour in all His sons and daughters. Achieving this has its fair share of challenges, especially in regard to forgiveness and judging others, but we should never stop pursuing it. Our goal is always His glory.

Reflections

Questions

- Are there any of your own particular attitudes or behaviours in which you have noticed a change taking place?

- Are you caught in a loop of tradition or frustration? Can you think of a way in which you could change your behaviour in order to improve the current situation?

- What can you learn from the widow who gave her last two coins into the offering box?

Practical application

Is there someone you haven't forgiven, or someone you are holding a grudge against? Start a prayer journal: write down the name of the person and the pain or hurt that has been done. Write a short prayer, expressing your honest feelings to God, and ask Him to help you deal with it. Come back to it again tomorrow and do the same thing again. This may be hard and extremely challenging, but it is absolutely necessary for spiritual growth.

Prayer

Father, I am thankful that because You have forgiven me, judgement has been removed. Help me, Lord, not to be judgemental but to show others the same compassion and grace that You have shown to me. Thank You for carrying all of my hurt. Please help me to develop an attitude of forgiveness and to let go of any past pain or resentment that I might still be holding on to. Teach me to love as You do. Amen.

8

The visible aspect of attitude

*First clean the inside of the cup and the plate, that
the outside also may be clean.*
(Matthew 23:26)

The Father's desire for us is that we become 'conformed to
the image of [the] Son' (Romans 8:29). Isn't that our goal too,
to become more Christlike? In order for that to happen we
need to align our behaviour and attitude with His, and the
only way to achieve this is to walk with Him, listen to Him
and learn from Him. Bringing about a change in how we
think and act comes through the renewing of our mind;[30] a
transformation that is only possible by the Spirit of God:

> And we all, with unveiled face, beholding the glory of
> the Lord, are being transformed into the same image
> from one degree of glory to another. For this comes
> from the Lord who is the Spirit.
> (2 Corinthians 3:18)

Bit by bit, day by day, we are being changed by the power of
God for His glory. This is great news for us, but not so great
for the devil, who will try to disrupt this change at every
opportunity. He will challenge our actions and reactions

---

[30] Romans 12:2.

constantly, and will tempt us to choose his way. He knows the weak spots to go for and he will exploit them fully.

Temptation comes to all of us in various shapes and forms, and what tempts me won't necessarily tempt you. We all have different weaknesses, which in most cases are not sinful of themselves. It's not sinful to be tempted by a nice slice of chocolate cake, but it does become an issue when it turns into constant gorging. There is no sin in buying a ticket to watch football or rugby and so on, but when the Sunday match starts to take precedence over church fellowship, there's a problem. One of the greatest weapons the devil has is temptation, but when he tried to tempt Jesus, he experienced his greatest failure.

Before the start of His ministry, 'Jesus was led up by the Spirit into the wilderness to be tempted by the devil' (Matthew 4:1). Temptation is sly and subtle, often creeping in slowly. It is cunning in approach, using something simple to lure us in. Jesus had been fasting for forty days and nights and the Bible tells us He was hungry. The devil saw an opening, came alongside Him, and said, 'If you are the Son of God, command these stones to become loaves of bread' (Matthew 4:3).

The thing about spiritual fasting is that it is always accompanied by prayer, and no one comes out of forty solitary days communing with God in a weakened spiritual state. The body may have been hungry, but the spirit was full. Jesus could immediately see what the devil was trying, and so, with words from the Scriptures, He answered, 'Man shall not live by bread alone, but by every word that comes from the mouth of God' (Matthew 4:4).

The second and third temptations were much less subtle, as the devil tried to appeal to ego and status, which was a complete misjudgement of the character of Jesus. Can the same be said when the tempter comes to us? Has he misjudged our character, or are we misjudging his? We need to be so careful with what we allow to have an influence over our behaviour. For the most part, each of us will be aware of where our weaknesses lie (there may be some still undiscovered), but we need to ask God to help strengthen our defences so that not even the toe of temptation can get in the door.

Having overcome temptation, Jesus spoke with authority to the tempter:

> 'Be gone, Satan! For it is written,
> "You shall worship the Lord your God
> and him only shall you serve."'
> Then the devil left him, and behold, angels came and
> were ministering to him.
> (Matthew 4:10-11)

Keeping our focus solely on Jesus and allowing Him to strengthen our mind, we can address the devil with confidence, telling him to 'be gone'. Jesus was mentally strong when combating the devil's advances, so we need to 'be renewed in the spirit of [our] minds' (Ephesians 4:23) to contend with every kind of temptation that Satan offers.

To be Christlike takes time, because transformation is not instantaneous, but is a process that develops through the understanding of God's Word. Knowledge enhances strength, a spiritual strength of the mind. As we grow in knowing more about Jesus and His character, the more we change inwardly to become like Him:

> Put on the new self, which is being renewed in
> knowledge after the image of its creator.
> (Colossians 3:10)

Old ways of thinking and behaving are left behind as we pursue a new focus, which is achieved through the power of God's Spirit working within our spirit. This 'new self' is visible in our walk and in our talk, and it is the evidence of our faith. For better or worse, whatever is happening on the inside will be seen on the outside.

I think it is fair to say that, at some point, we all wonder how other people perceive us. For me, those kinds of thoughts tend to ebb and flow, with times of being quite anxious about it to times of being completely unconcerned. Those times of feeling anxious often come from low self-confidence, or wanting desperately to fit in, which has its roots in a fundamental need to be liked.

You may have heard it said that it doesn't matter what other people think, it only matters what God thinks, and in certain ways that's true. In our daily living, though, it does matter what others see. Do they see a child of God? Do the talk and the walk match up; do they reflect the character of Christ? We are to 'walk in wisdom towards outsiders' (Colossians 4:5), so that when they look at us they see a true reflection of who God is. Our aim as Christians is not simply to fit in and go with the flow, but to stand up and stand strong, knowing who we are in Christ. We generally interact with hundreds of people on a yearly basis and our faith is seen through every action and every word. Communicating is a big part of daily life for many of us, and we need to be more aware of the words that we say and the effect they can have.

A verse that I was drawn to recently, says, 'And Samuel grew, and the LORD was with him and let none of his words fall to the ground' (1 Samuel 3:19). The phrase that really struck me was, 'and let none of his words fall to the ground', which produced a visual of words being carried through the air. It sounds a bit strange, I know, but just imagine it for a moment. Imagine seeing all the words you speak literally going out from your mouth, and watching as they either go up, go out or go down. All the words of praise, thanksgiving, petition and intercession are carried upwards to heaven. Every word that tells others of the love of God and the work of the cross, and every word spoken in kindness, encouragement and support is carried on the breath of the Spirit and absorbed by the listener. But every unkind word, every half-truth, words of gossip and those of no worth just fall to the ground. As you imagine that happening, how much of your conversation would just be lying at your feet?

It is quite a sobering thought, but it is something we have control over, for we can choose to use our words in all the ways God intended. One of the saddest verses in the story of Samuel is near the beginning, which tells us that 'the word of the LORD was rare in those days' (1 Samuel 3:1). In Samuel, however, God found someone who was willing to listen and willing to carry His words to those who needed to hear.

Samuel opened the doors of the house of the Lord, inviting people to come and hear. We need to open the doors of our heart and mind and allow God's Word to reside there, so that when we open the door of our mouth, only words of worth come out.

Attitude is on the tongue

It is frightening how something as small as the tongue has the potential to do so much damage. From a careless word to a blatant lie, one person's life can be forever altered by the words of another. 'How great a forest is set ablaze by such a small fire!' (James 3:5). Think about the sarcastic word, the thoughtless remark, the curt comment – all this comes from the same tongue that gives thanks to God and blesses His name. How can this be? Can fresh and salt water flow from the same spring?[31] This is the old self in battle with the new self, and it is one of the many reasons why we need the power of the Holy Spirit working within us. It is also why we need to hand our words over to God every day so that they may be good, helpful, encouraging, respectful and, above all, bring glory and honour to Him:

---

[31] James 3:11.

> Set a guard, O LORD, over my mouth;
> keep watch over the door of my lips!
> (Psalm 141:3)

Christians represent a higher authority at all times, in public and in private. Regardless of whether we are a billboard Christian with an extrovert personality or a bumper-sticker Christian with a quieter demeanour, all that we do and say reflects on the name of the Lord Jesus. Our commission is to draw people to Jesus, not drive them further away. As ambassadors for Christ, we have been entrusted with the message of reconciliation.[32] With this in mind, we should try to avoid getting dragged into futile discussions and unproductive arguments. Instead, our aim should be to 'speak evil of no one, to avoid quarrelling, to be gentle, and to show perfect courtesy towards all people' (Titus 3:2).

When a conversation is going nowhere but downhill, in order to exercise grace, we may need to exercise restraint and excuse ourselves from the discussion. One of my favourite proverbs says, 'Whoever keeps his mouth and his tongue keeps himself out of trouble' (Proverbs 21:23), which basically means, if in doubt keep it zipped and you won't get into bother! We are to be respectful of one another and use our conversation to build each other up, not tear each other down. When we are in discussion with someone who opposes our point of view, we need to remember that a gentle answer and a calm tone can achieve so much more than a harsh response.

Gentleness is a fruit of the Spirit[33] and is in opposition to speaking harshly, cruelly or quarrelling. I see this as a perfect example of why we should never 'quench the Spirit' (1 Thessalonians 5:19). I sometimes wonder if we appreciate the extent to which the Spirit of God helps us in our daily lives, and in every conversation that we have. We will never be in

---

[32] 2 Corinthians 5:18.
[33] Galatians 5:22-23.

agreement with everyone we meet, but we can be courteous to all who cross our path.

A measured attitude

> *Give, and it will be given to you. Good measure,*
> *pressed down, shaken together, running over, will be*
> *put into your lap.*
> *(Luke 6:38)*

Jesus taught the realities of living a measured life, which we looked at in the previous chapter through the teachings found in Matthew 7. He said:

> Judge not, that you be not judged. For with the judgement you pronounce you will be judged, and with the measure you use it will be measured to you. (Matthew 7:1-2)

In Luke's record of these teachings, we also hear Jesus say:

> Condemn not, and you will not be condemned; forgive, and you will be forgiven; give, and it will be given to you.
> (Luke 6:37-38)

Measure for measure. Judgement and forgiveness. Stop and consider for a moment what that means in your life. It is not an easy thought, but none of us wants a large measure of judgement and a small measure of forgiveness. We want to be given the good measure of good things, 'pressed down, shaken together, [and] running over' (Luke 6:38).

In the life of the Christian, a right attitude in good measure is vital for treating people in a right manner, regardless of their actions. As mentioned at the beginning of this topic, a right attitude comes from a place of genuine love:

a love for our brothers and sisters in Christ, and a love for those who haven't found Him yet.

> By this all people will know that you are my disciples,
> if you have love for one another.
> (John 13:35)

Having a right attitude enables us to serve God 'in a manner worthy of the Lord, fully pleasing to him, bearing fruit in every good work and increasing in the knowledge of God' (Colossians 1:10). This is what God deserves from us, but we can only serve Him in a right manner when our actions are in line with the attitude of Jesus.

Reflections

Questions

- What does it mean for you to be 'renewed in the spirit of your [mind]' (Ephesians 4:23) in order to contend with temptation?

- In what circumstances do you find yourself wondering what others might be thinking about you? Have you found a way of dealing with that?

- We could all benefit from having a lock on the door of our mouth at times. In what kind of conversations have you found it most difficult to exercise restraint? How do you feel about walking away from a conversation that is going nowhere and simply leaving it in the hands of God?

Practical application

Think about the old self and the new self. First, note down any part of the old you that still needs to be worked on – for example, what you recognise as weak spots – and hand these areas over to God. Second, note down what you see as the new you and ask God to continue to strengthen and grow these new attitudes and behaviour.

Prayer

Father God, I want to be more like Jesus in all that I say and do. I pray that as I walk with You and listen to You, my mind would be renewed bit by bit, day by day, by the power of the Spirit within me. Help me to keep my focus solely on You so that I can fight against the temptations that come my way. Help me, Lord, to be mindful in every conversation, and if my words are not helpful, then help me to be quiet. In Jesus' name. Amen.

9

Understanding our purpose

But rise and stand upon your feet, for I have appeared
to you for this purpose, to appoint you as a servant
and witness.
(Acts 26:16)

Everyone needs purpose, because purpose gives our lives meaning and direction. It is a basic human need, and people all across the world are continually searching for it. Purpose raises questions that many people have asked over the years. What is the meaning of life; what is it all about? What is my place in the world? Value and worth are constantly questioned, for among all the needs that we have, we also need to be needed.

Many moons ago, while studying psychology, my fellow students and I were introduced to a renowned psychologist by the name of Abraham Maslow. Maslow had been intrigued by the strong mental growth of individuals, and so he studied the basic needs that every human requires in order to live a fulfilled life. Following his study, he produced a five-stage model entitled 'Hierarchy of Needs' which consisted of the following:

Stage 1: Physiological needs (food, water, warmth, rest).
Stage 2: Safety needs (a home, work, resources, etc).

Stage 3: Belonging and love needs (relationships, etc).
Stage 4: Esteem needs (worth, respect, etc).
Stage 5: Self-actualisation (finding meaning and fulfilling one's full potential).[34]

The idea behind the model is that when stage 1 is achieved, we move up to address the needs in stage 2. When these are achieved, then more needs emerge, and we continue to grow and be fulfilled; step by step, stage by stage. In 1954, reaching one's full potential was the final stage, but in the mid 1960s Maslow discovered something beyond this, which he was compelled to explore. He called it Transcendence, as it was a peak experience which led to a place of enlightenment. In his book, *Religions, Values, and Peak-Experiences*, he writes:

> The peak-experience itself can often meaningfully be called a 'little death,' and a rebirth in various senses ... Man has a higher and transcendent nature, and this is part of his essence, i.e., his biological nature as a member of a species which has evolved ... it looks quite probable that the peak-experience may be the model of the religious revelation or the religious illumination or conversion which has played so great a role in the history of religions.[35]

I am fascinated by what Maslow discovered, and yet at the same time I am not in the least surprised that he found there to be more to Man than man itself – or, on a personal basis, there is more to me than just me.

There is a higher nature within each one of us which is ignited by the higher power of the Creator, and Him alone. When we discover Him and accept Him as Lord and Saviour

[34] See www.simplypsychology.org/maslow.html (accessed 19th April 2024).
[35] Abraham H Maslow, *Religions, Values, and Peak-Experiences* (Victoria, BC: Rare Treasure Editions, 2021), pp 12, 13, 41.

of our lives, our hierarchy of needs is covered by His all-encompassing providence:

> God will supply every need of yours according to his
> riches in glory in Christ Jesus.
> (Philippians 4:19)

We find warmth in the Father's love; we find rest and safety within His arms; we find a place of belonging where we have immense value and worth; in Him, we find the meaning of life and our purpose in this world.

As a child of God, have you come to understand your purpose? Are you living out your full potential for His glory? Have your thoughts been taken to a higher place of marvel and beauty, or has the 'enlightenment' of this world only served to make things darker? This is not an unusual thing to happen, because experiencing God's truth can often lead to even more questions.

In Psalm 73, Asaph had questions, and if we read this psalm from the beginning, we see how brutally honest Asaph was with himself and with God. He knew that God was 'good to those who are pure in heart', and that was what he wanted to be, but the thoughts within his heart and mind were failing him:

> As for me, my feet had almost stumbled,
> my steps had nearly slipped.
> For I was envious of the arrogant
> when I saw the prosperity of the wicked.
> (Psalm 73:2-3)

Asaph's thoughts took him to a dark place and he wondered why he even tried to do what was right when there seemed to be no justice for those who did wrong. In fact, they appeared to prosper, and even though they spoke out against God, no trouble came their way.

Asaph asked himself a question that many still ask today: 'Have I lived my life in vain?' All these thoughts brought his spirit low, and he says, 'But when I thought how to understand this, it seemed to me a wearisome task' (Psalm 73:16). Notice the word 'seemed'. Asaph was about to find clarity for all his thoughts.

So what was it that revived his spirit, calmed his mind and stopped him from falling further into apathy? 'It *seemed* to me a wearisome task, *until* I went into the sanctuary of God' (vv16-17, my emphasis). The presence of God changes everything. In His presence we find our strength, our hope and our purpose. In His presence we find the assurance that our life is never lived in vain when we live it for Him.

As I said earlier, everyone needs purpose, because purpose gives our lives meaning and direction. God is the One who brings true meaning to all that we do, and He is the One who directs us in finding His plan and purpose for our lives.

Light for the darkness

In Chapter Two, as we looked at the I AM statements, we heard Jesus say, 'I am the light of the world' (John 8:12). Jesus is the light in this dark world, but how is that light seen if Jesus is not physically present in the world? The light is seen (or should be seen) through every disciple of Christ, for although Jesus is not physically present, He is spiritually present in the lives of His followers. This is why He said:

> You are the light of the world. A city set on a hill cannot be hidden. Nor do people light a lamp and put it under a basket, but on a stand, and it gives light to all in the house.
> (Matthew 5:14-15)

Jesus spoke these words while sitting on the side of a mountain, which was a great place to illustrate His point. It hadn't been too long before this that the devil had taken Jesus to a high mountain to show Him the kingdoms of the world (Matthew 4:8). Jesus knew only too well how dark the world had become, and He also knew that not everyone would welcome the light because they wouldn't want their deeds in full view. This is, however, the very reason that He wants us to shine, because sin needs to be addressed and it needs to be dealt with. Jesus is asking that we illuminate the truth so that the lost can find the path out of the darkness.

Light is not a subtle thing, and maybe you're thinking that you don't want to be a bold and obvious bright light. Jesus is not asking us to be a disco ball or a strobe light – we don't want to give people a headache – but we do need to shine, so don't be heavy-handed with the dimmer switch:

> Let your light shine before others, so that they may see your good works and give glory to your Father who is in heaven.
> (Matthew 5:16)

In order for us to be able to reflect the light of Jesus, we need to be continually looking to Him through spiritual eyes. 'The eye is the lamp of the body. So, if your eye is healthy, your whole body will be full of light' (Matthew 6:22). The eyes are such an amazing part of the body, with each one having more than a hundred million light-sensitive cells.[36] These cells want to pull in as much light as possible in order that we might see clearly.

Anyone with diminishing sight will tell you how precious it is to have healthy eyes. Likewise, our spiritual eyes need to be healthy and clear in order to see all that the Lord reveals to us as we live out our daily lives for Him. Jesus is the source of pure light and we want to pull in as much of that as we possibly can. Luke tells us that the Lord said to His disciples, 'Blessed are the eyes that see what you see!' (Luke 10:23).

---

[36] retinauk.org.uk/information-and-support/about-inherited-sight-loss/eye-structure/ (accessed 19th April 2024)

Jesus was not only letting them see who He truly was; He was also letting them see the Father and the truth of the kingdom.

In the second letter to the Corinthians, the apostle Paul says, 'For God, who said, "Let light shine out of darkness", has shone in our hearts to give the light of the knowledge of the glory of God in the face of Jesus Christ' (2 Corinthians 4:6). When we keep our eyes firmly focused on Jesus, our whole body will be full of light.

Focused with purpose

After His death, Jesus appeared and spoke with His disciples on several different occasions. Before His ascension into heaven, He gave them a very clear directive, often referred to as the great commission:

> Go therefore and make disciples of all nations, baptizing them in the name of the Father and of the Son and of the Holy Spirit, teaching them to observe all that I have commanded you. And behold, I am with you always, to the end of the age.
> (Matthew 28:19-20)

This was it. The training wheels were coming off and it was time to move forward, completely focused with purpose. The time had come for all people everywhere to hear the gospel of Jesus. I imagine that amid the excitement of taking the gospel to a new and varied audience, there was also the feeling of being overwhelmed by such a daunting task. They were not being sent out unequipped, though, for Jesus had 'opened their minds to understand the Scriptures' (Luke 24:45), and soon they would be 'clothed with power from on high' (Luke 24:49).

This same commission remains today, and the task can still feel daunting and overwhelming at times, but we are no less equipped than those first disciples. The power of the Holy Spirit resides within every believer, and the Lord continues to open up the Scriptures to us. His Word gives us the strength and the courage to speak to all who will listen.

We don't even have to go far to start our mission. The apostles were to begin in Jerusalem, right in the very place they already were. Reaching people who need Jesus can start in our own home, our own street, our own community. At times this can be easy and at other times more difficult. Maybe you feel that you would love to be able to talk to others about Jesus but you feel nervous or anxious, or even embarrassed. It could be that like Moses you feel that your words would be inadequate for the task. If that is the case, then God's reply to this worry can give confidence to each one of us: 'Go, and I will be with your mouth and teach you what you shall speak' (Exodus 4:12).

In Exodus 3 we are told that God was sending Moses to the people of Israel because He had compassion on them. Likewise, when Jesus came and looked out across the crowds, His heart was moved and 'he had compassion for them, because they were harassed and helpless, like sheep without a shepherd' (Matthew 9:36). As God sent Moses, Jesus sends us to bring hope to those who are lost by bringing His light into very dark places.

Having Jesus as our Saviour means having His light dwell within us, which leads us to a responsibility for that light to be seen. Even if we struggle to find words to say, we can always find actions to show, because part of letting your light shine is 'so that [others] may see your good works and give glory to your Father who is in heaven' (Matthew 5:16). What we do is just as important as what we say. We are to show kindness, show gentleness, show patience, show goodness, show love, for:

> If you pour yourself out for the hungry
> and satisfy the desire of the afflicted,
> then shall your light rise in the darkness

and your gloom be as the noonday.
And the LORD will guide you continually.
(Isaiah 58:10-11)

Show and tell

Throughout His ministry, Jesus continually revealed the truth
of the Word of God that had been spoken to the Israelites
down through the generations. Jesus delivered these truths
through parables, fulfilling the prophecy, 'I will open my
mouth in parables; I will utter what has been hidden since the
foundation of the world' (Matthew 13:35). God sent the Son
so that the secrets of heaven would reach the ears of every
person on earth. Jesus revealed them first to His disciples and
through them the mystery of the gospel spread throughout
the world:

> For nothing is hidden that will not be made manifest,
> nor is anything secret that will not be known and come
> to light.
> (Luke 8:17)

This verse is often quoted in regard to sinful behaviour, that
those who commit dark deeds will be judged in the full light
of God's courtroom. While this is indeed true, it is not the
context in which Jesus was speaking. In this instance, Jesus
was talking to the disciples; these words were for them and
are for every disciple after them. Part of the process of the
ministry of Jesus was to build up, strengthen and equip these
faithful followers to carry on His ministry. Even though they
didn't always understand what was happening, each
instruction that Jesus gave them was a prelude to the great
commission: 'What I tell you in the dark, say in the light, and
what you hear whispered, proclaim on the housetops'
(Matthew 10:27).

Day by day, lesson by lesson, the secrets of the kingdom
of God and the will of the Father were being revealed

through the Word, which was Jesus. As we read the Bible, God continues to reveal the secrets of His Word to those who truly seek Him: 'You will seek me and find me, when you seek me with all your heart' (Jeremiah 29:13). It is such an incredible experience to read God's Word and have it come alive in your mind and in the depths of your spirit; to read a verse and literally feel like a light has been switched on, and the truth within the lines becomes clear. This is what happens when our spirit unites with God's Spirit:

> But, as it is written,
> 'What no eye has seen, nor ear heard,
> nor the heart of man imagined,
> what God has prepared for those who love him' –
> these things God has revealed to us through the Spirit.
> For the Spirit searches everything, even the depths of God.
> (1 Corinthians 2:9-10)

What the Father whispers to us in the quietness, we then proclaim; what He tells us in the dark, we say in the light, for we are His light. Our purpose is to spread the wonder and the hope of the gospel to everyone who will listen. God's Word may be a mystery to those who don't yet believe, but it is a secret that we have permission to tell, so don't be afraid to pass it on.

Shake the dust

Passing it on is not always going to be straightforward, and it definitely will not always be easy. As we share the good news of Jesus, whether that is through everyday conversation or organised evangelism, some people will be ready to listen and some won't want to know. Rather than digging in our heels with a determination not to budge until our message has been accepted, Jesus says, 'If anyone will not receive you or listen to your words, shake off the dust from your feet when you leave that house or town' (Matthew 10:14).

This verse takes me back to a time of street evangelism, when we would go from town to town sharing the good news of the gospel. Each time someone was completely uninterested or hostile, we would literally shake our feet as they walked away. I have no doubt that some folk thought we were doing some kind of weird religious dance! But why would the Lord tell us to do this seemingly strange thing?

We have probably all had someone say to us, 'Just shake it off,' meaning whatever another person has said or done that has upset or annoyed you, don't let it get under your skin. The Lord knows that not everyone who hears the gospel will accept it; a lot will turn away or even ridicule those who speak it. As with His disciples, Jesus does not want us to be distracted or discouraged by those who aren't ready to receive the good news. So when someone is not interested in what we have to say, we simply shake it off and move on.

There are people all around us who are searching for the one true God. They don't always realise it at the time, but they know that they are looking for something – something different, something better, something real. These are the people Jesus wants us to reach. We are seed-sowers, but we never know for sure what type of soil we are getting, and not all ground is ready to receive the seed. The Christian often falls into the trap of feeling that they have failed in some way if the person they are sharing the gospel with doesn't give their life to God. We need to remember that our commission is to go and tell, not go and save. Jesus is the Saviour. We simply sow God's wonderful truths into the lives of others and the Holy Spirit works through those truths to convict the hearer of their need for salvation. Some people will get saved the first time they hear God's good news; others may take a lifetime. So when you feel a conversation is going nowhere, don't be afraid to shake the dust off and walk on, for there are many others just waiting to hear life-changing news.

Different tactics

Sharing the wonderful news of Jesus is as exciting as it is challenging. God, by His Spirit, can guide us to people from a variety of backgrounds. When we understand our audience, we can better explain the wonders of God's kingdom and the power that He has to change their life on a personal level.

In the book of Acts, we read of three missionary journeys that the apostle Paul embarked on. His travels took him through Syria, Asia Minor (Turkey), Greece and Cyprus (to name but a few places). Here he encountered Jews, Romans and Greeks, each with their own belief system, and for the latter two, their own deities. On one particular occasion, Paul and Barnabas were in a town called Lystra (southern Turkey), an area heavily influenced by both Greek and Roman culture. They had been preaching the gospel and engaging with the people when Paul noticed a crippled man listening intently to all that was being said. Recognising that this man had faith to be made well, Paul told him to stand up.

When the people witnessed the man standing up and walking at Paul's command, they thought that their gods had come down among them. They believed that Barnabas was Zeus and that Paul was Hermes. Addressing the people, Paul declared, 'We also are men, of like nature with you, and we bring you good news, that you should turn from these vain things to a living God, who made the heaven and the earth and the sea and all that is in them' (Acts 14:15).

They had come to show the people a real living God as opposed to mythical deities who could do nothing for them. The people of Lystra served gods whom they believed sat in a heavenly place, but Paul wanted them to see the God who actually *made* the heavens!

Talking to people and sharing the gospel with those who have completely different views or beliefs can be difficult, and it can sometimes mean having to adjust the focal point. When Paul preached to the Jews, he referred to the Torah and their forefather, Abraham. In Asia Minor, with Greco-

Roman influence, he referred to the living God, the Creator of all things. Paul never changed the message of the gospel of Christ, but he learned to adjust the way in which it was told, depending on the audience. Every person deserves to hear of God's salvation; we just need to find the best way to tell them about it.

Sometimes light, sometimes salt

Telling people about Jesus and the amazing love of God is equal parts word and action. Sometimes we go and tell; sometimes we go and do. We are walking, talking influencers, and as we have seen through the parable of the leaven, we can have a positive influence on others by the power of the Spirit within us. Jesus pointed to this influence again when He said, 'You are the salt of the earth' (Matthew 5:13).

Salt has an effect on everything it touches. It holds back decay, it stings an open wound but can help it heal quicker, it creates thirst and it can add flavour. Through this verse, Jesus is telling us of our purpose and value in this world.

Jesus came as the hope to a dying and decaying world, and He has passed the mantle on to those who love and serve Him. We are salt in the midst of decay and a salve to the wounded soul. We are a means of creating a spiritual thirst in those who don't know Jesus, and we are flavour enhancers of all the goodness of God:

Oh, taste and see that the LORD is good!
(Psalm 34:8)

We are packed full of salty goodness, but that salt needs to be shaken out and used. In the same way that a light is of no use if it is hidden under a basket, salt does no good just sitting inside the container. We need to grind the salt-mill and let it spill out as we walk and as we talk:

> Let your speech always be gracious, seasoned with
> salt, so that you may know how you ought to answer
> each person.
> (Colossians 4:6)

This is a verse of instruction with a reason, but that little word 'how' caused me some thought. I wondered how sprinkling my conversation with salt and grace would help me to know 'how' to answer someone.

First things first, I looked at the verse in the original Greek, which told me, 'Your speech, always in grace, having been seasoned with salt, to know how it behoves you, each one to answer.' OK, so that didn't make things any clearer for me at all. In fact, I am now looking at a Bible dictionary to find out the meaning of 'behoves'. Translated from the Greek word – *dei* – it means, necessary; it is what *must* happen, what is *absolutely* necessary. This is when the lightbulb in my head switched on: Grace + Salt + Necessary answers.

How we answer someone is important. We are to be courteous, not curt; we are to be helpful, not harsh. What comes out of our mouth should be 'such as is good for building up, as fits the occasion, that it may give grace to those who hear' (Ephesians 4:29). A gentle answer, a calm tone, an encouraging word – these can achieve so much more than an unthoughtful comment.

Do you remember a time when you felt a bit low, questioned a decision or doubted your own efforts? How good did it feel to talk with someone who boosted your confidence or lifted your spirits? The ability to make someone feel good, feel positive or feel better is a wonderful trait to have, and it starts with grace and salt. We are surrounded by people who are hurting; troubled souls with anxiety and fears, all looking for a little help, a little hope and a lot of understanding. They do not need unnecessary platitudes. They need necessary answers. As we let the Holy Spirit guide our conversations, we can spread a little bit of God's grace into someone else's life.

Beware of tasteless salt

Answering someone in a harsh or curt tone or handing out unnecessary platitudes is as beneficial as tasteless salt on a plate of food. After Jesus had referred to His followers as salt of the earth, He added this stark truth:

> If salt has lost its taste, how shall its saltiness be restored? It is no longer good for anything except to be thrown out and trampled under people's feet. (Matthew 5:13).

Salt will always be salt, but it has the potential to lose its effectiveness. We need to be so careful not to let outside influences contaminate our purpose. The world should not be changing us; we should be changing the world. What God has created within us should not be allowed to get trampled under conformity. We were meticulously crafted with thought, with care and with expectation. We were fashioned and created with purpose, and when we allow the Holy Spirit to fill our life, we become the effective salt and light that Jesus declared us to be.

Your life has meaning; *you* have meaning, and as a witness and servant of Christ there is kingdom work to be done which has your name on it, so in all things 'remain faithful to the Lord with steadfast purpose' (Acts 11:23).

Reflections

Questions

- As you think about your purpose and potential, what are some outside influences that could hinder these?

- Sharing the gospel can feel daunting, especially with family and friends. How might you be able to 'show' them the gospel alongside 'telling' them?

- As you think about the concepts of being salt and light – how do you see this being worked out in your daily life?

Practical application

The apostle Paul used different tactics to share the same gospel when talking with various groups of people. Think about the different people you come into contact with and note down some ideas of how you might present the gospel to them specifically.

Prayer

Lord Jesus, I want to fulfil my potential and walk purposely for You. Open my eyes and my mind to fully understand what it means to be salt and light in this world. Guide and direct me as I talk to people about You, and give me the right words to say in every conversation. In Your name I pray. Amen.

10
Teaching us how to serve

Taking the form of a servant ... he humbled himself by
becoming obedient.
(Philippians 2:7-8)

Jesus did not only teach with words, but He also taught through action. So in order for us to truly understand service, we need to watch and learn from the One who remained faithful with steadfast purpose. Jesus showed us how to live an obedient life, a life of purpose. This life involved constant prayer and fellowship with God the Father, and it involved immoveable commitment to His eternal plan. Jesus was completely focused on the will of the Father and the work of the eternal kingdom.

The servant heart of Jesus is beautifully portrayed during the final Passover meal with His disciples. This was a private meal in a borrowed guest room, so there was no one playing the part of host and there were no servants to serve. It is evident that not one of the disciples was prepared to take on this role, so they all sat down around the table with their dusty feet. Jesus, always the teacher, saw that another lesson needed to be taught, so He got up from the table:

> He laid aside his outer garments, and taking a towel,
> tied it round his waist. Then he poured water into a

basin and began to wash the disciples' feet and to wipe
them with the towel that was wrapped round him.
(John 13:4-5)

Peter could not believe what was happening, and the image
of the Messiah kneeling before him was just too much for
him to comprehend. When Jesus came to him with the basin,
he was indignant and said, 'You shall never wash my feet'
(John 13:8). Peter was someone who always seemed to act on
impulse and instinct, but in that moment Jesus wanted him
to be still and to learn.

We can all be a bit like Peter at times, with our impulsive
words and actions, but if we want to learn from Jesus, we
need quiet hearts, not busy minds. Teaching always goes a lot
easier when there are no interruptions, for it allows the full
lesson to be explained before we jump in with misguided
thoughts.

After Jesus had finished washing the feet of each disciple,
He sat down once more. He asked if they understood what
He had done, and then said:

> You call me Teacher and Lord, and you are right, for
> so I am. If I then, your Lord and Teacher, have
> washed your feet, you also ought to wash one
> another's feet. For I have given you an example, that
> you also should do just as I have done to you.
> (John 13:13-15)

Jesus chose the humblest of acts to portray the heart of a
servant. He had heard discussions and questions among the
disciples on a number of occasions as to who was the
greatest, and His message was consistent. 'Whoever would be
great among you must be your servant ... even as the Son of
Man came not to be served but to serve' (Matthew 20:26, 28).
At this meal He tells them again, 'A servant is not greater
than his master, nor is a messenger greater than the one who
sent him' (John 13:16). There is no hierarchy among God's

children; there are no blue-collar and white-collar Christians. We are one people; we are all equal and we are all servants of the King.

If the Lord can bend down in humble service, then each of us can take the basin and towel and bow in loving service to one another. Kingdom work is active work and we all need to get involved, and as Jesus said, 'If you know these things, blessed are you if you do them' (John 13:17). God does not want us standing on the sidelines simply cheering others on with shouts of, 'Keep up the good work!' and, 'You're doing a great job!' God wants every one of us to be active. Are we making ourselves available to God's will and allowing Him to use us to our full potential? There is no shortage of good work to be done, for there is so much need all around us. People need kindness; they need genuine care and thoughtfulness. We need to let the love of God within us be borne out in practical ways by actively seeking opportunities to serve, for in serving others, we are serving Christ:

> For I was hungry and you gave me food, I was thirsty and you gave me drink, I was a stranger and you welcomed me, I was naked and you clothed me, I was sick and you visited me, I was in prison and you came to me.
> (Matthew 25:35-36)

It is God's will that we care for the poor, the outcast, the mistreated and abused. It is His will that we feed the hungry, bring peace to the troubled, relief to the burdened and comfort to the distressed. Through every conversation and every action we have an opportunity to serve, and through serving we bring glory to God. We are the hands and feet of the Lord in this time, bringing His gentleness, kindness and compassion to those around us. He has given each of us the ability and the resources for good and wonderful works. Most importantly, he has given us His Spirit:

> I am sending the promise of my Father upon you ...
> you [will be] clothed with power from on high.
> (Luke 24:49)

Ready for service

The purpose, plan and will of God are always in motion and we are expected to be instruments in His work. What is not expected is that we do God's work in our own strength. The Father Himself will clothe us with power, enabling us to carry out the work of the kingdom. A plumber doesn't go out to fix a leak with a roll of sticky tape, and a gardener doesn't trim a hedge with a penknife; both go out with the right tools for the job. In the same way, God equips us with exactly what we need so that we can serve Him with confidence.

Every Christian should be in no doubt about the power of the Spirit within them. This is not something that might, maybe, possibly happen to a select few. This is a promise of the Son, from the Father, to every believer and follower of Christ. This is the Trinity in motion for the work of the kingdom. The Father began the plan, the Son became the plan and the Holy Spirit continues the plan through each one of us. We have power within, power from on high.

Regardless of how we feel in ourselves, God does not send us out in weakness; He sends us out in strength. The power of the Spirit stirs up courage, grants us deeper access to the things of God and increases knowledge so that we can spread the good news with boldness, serve the Lord with confidence and face opposition without fear. To be clothed with power is to be dressed for success as we undertake the work of God:

> For we are his workmanship, created in Christ Jesus
> for good works, which God prepared beforehand, that
> we should walk in them.
> (Ephesians 2:10)

This verse is taken from a letter that the apostle Paul wrote to the church at Ephesus. It was a letter of thanksgiving and of encouragement. In this verse, Paul is encouraging his readers to walk in the work that God has prepared. If you read through Paul's other letters, you will notice that he uses the term 'walk' quite a lot in his writing: 'walk in love' (Ephesians 5:2), 'walk as children of light' (Ephesians 5:8), 'walk in newness of life' (Romans 6:4), 'walk in wisdom' (Colossians 4:5). You will also notice that when he wasn't walking, he was running![37] The image we get from this is of a Christian life that is in perpetual motion. That is not to imply that we do not rest, but rather that we do not become stagnant in service. God created us 'in Christ Jesus for good works' so our commitment to Him is to walk in them continually and to be an active people for an active God.

A phrase that I heard quite often when I was younger was, 'Stop sitting there twiddling your thumbs and give me a hand, please.' I wasn't even sure what 'twiddling' was, but apparently I was quite good at it. Solomon tells us, 'A slack hand causes poverty, but the hand of the diligent makes rich' (Proverbs 10:4).

Being active helps us to avoid falling into a lifestyle of idleness and laziness. Being idle doesn't get the work done, and being lazy only serves to slow it down. Jesus is fully aware of this lack of commitment as He points out this truth: 'The harvest is plentiful, but the labourers are few' (Matthew 9:37). As individuals and as the Church, we are not to be slack but diligent in the work of the Lord.

The work of the kingdom is vast and varied, and when we are part of God's family, we have a part to play in the family business. There will be times when we work alone on specific tasks, and there will be times when we are called to work alongside our brothers and sisters. God has given us gifts and talents to be used in His service, so it would be a disservice

---

[37] See 1 Corinthians 9:24.

to let them go to waste. The Lord Jesus became 'a merciful and faithful high priest in the service of God' (Hebrews 2:17), and we must now fulfil our calling of service and walk in the good works that He has prepared for us to do.

Has God laid a particular work on your heart, something that He has purposed for you to do? Have you started yet or are you still procrastinating, weighing up the pros and cons? Maybe you have started and are currently somewhere in the middle of it, but other things are calling for your attention. Some interruptions are genuine, but we need to be wary of things that try to take us away from God's immediate purpose.

When God shows us His will, He also goes before us to prepare a way for His will to be done. It is true, though, that even with the greatest of intentions, we can often get distracted easily. We can be convinced to stop what we're doing, take a short break or attend to something far less important. We need to be watchful for distractions and not let them pull us away from His purpose. That means staying focused and letting God guide us to where He needs us to be. However, we shouldn't be surprised if where God is leading us is not where other people think we should be. Good always comes from the Father's good works, but sometimes those around us won't see that right away, and others may not be happy about the work at all. But, if God has laid something specific on our heart to do, then we should determine to stay resolute, trust His leading and stand firm against opposition.

Working against opposition

In the Old Testament we read the story of Nehemiah, who was distraught when he heard that Jerusalem's walls were in ruins and the gates destroyed by fire.[38] He cried, prayed and fasted until the Lord told him what to do. The walls and gates

---

[38] Nehemiah 1:3-4.

were to be rebuilt and Nehemiah would lead this charge. He got everything in order and then got to work, but not everyone was happy, and plans to disrupt the work began. Nehemiah recognised a distraction when he saw one:

> I sent messengers to them, saying, 'I am doing a great work and I cannot come down. Why should the work stop while I leave it and come down to you?'
> (Nehemiah 6:3)

Nehemiah was committed to what God had put into his heart to do, and he was determined that the work would not stop. God had a timetable and Nehemiah was working to it; when he came up against opposition, he prayed, 'O God, strengthen my hands' (Nehemiah 6:9). God's plan is the only one that we should be following, and when we do, He will give us the strength we need to fulfil it.

In step with God's timetable

Someone else who was more focused on following the plans of God rather than listening to the opposition of others was Mary. This is the same Mary we met previously, the sister of Lazarus and Martha, but on this occasion her actions caused quite a debate, which Matthew, Mark and John tell us about.[39]

This story took place in the week leading up to Passover, in the town of Bethany. Jesus and His disciples had been invited for a meal, and as they reclined around the table, Mary came to Jesus, broke open a jar of ointment and poured the contents on His head and feet. This pure act of love and worship to the Lord was met with anger from the disciples, and they turned on her saying, 'Why this waste? For this could have been sold for a large sum and given to the poor' (Matthew 26:8-9).

---

[39] Matthew 26:6-13; Mark 14:3-9; John 12:1-8.

It is understandable why the disciples were upset. Mary had used a costly ointment, and the amount she had used (a pound of pure nard worth 300 denarii)[40] equated to around a year's wages. This could truly have fed and clothed a lot of people. For Mary, this was something that had been laid on her heart to do, in this place and at this time. Jesus knew the significance of what she had done, and He spoke to the disciples, saying, 'Why do you trouble the woman? For she has done a beautiful thing to me' (Matthew 26:10).

Jesus was not making little of their concerns, but He did want them to focus on what was important in that moment: 'For you always have the poor with you, but you will not always have me' (Matthew 26:11). Jesus was telling them that there would be weeks and months and years ahead to look after the needy, but His time with them was drawing to a close, and that was where their focus should be at that moment.

In all of the different types of work and tasks to be done for the kingdom, there will be a lot of things (and people) that will try to hinder them. This is why it is so important to trust God and listen to the voice of His Spirit, which enables us to keep in step with His timetable:

> For everything there is a season, and a time for every
> matter under heaven.
> (Ecclesiastes 3:1)

The Lord's work

It is possible that you are reading this and wondering what exactly 'God's work' looks like in your life. As discussed earlier, the work to be done is vast and varied, but it all starts from the same place:

---

[40] John 12:3,5.

> You shall love the Lord your God with all your heart
> and with all your soul and with all your mind. This is
> the great and first commandment. And a second is like
> it: You shall love your neighbour as yourself.
> (Matthew 22:37-39)

When we care for the poor, the widow and the orphan, when
we feed the hungry, welcome the stranger, visit the sick and
help the hurting, we are carrying out the Lord's work. This is
what Jesus did as He ministered in the towns and villages,
from region to region. Jesus ministered in word and in action.
He broke down barriers in class, status and religious
affiliations, for in the kingdom of God they mean nothing.

In Luke 10, Jesus illustrates what it means to love without
barriers through the story of the Samaritan and his incredible
act of kindness. We are not told the name of the Samaritan,
nor are we told any specifics about the man that he helped.
The omission of these details tells us a lot about the kind of
attitude that Jesus wants us to have in serving Him. We don't
need to know someone's complete background or history in
order to offer them help. Genuine concern and compassion
look beyond the 'what' (social status, skin colour, religious
affiliation, lifestyle choice) and focus on the 'who' – someone
in need. This is the Father's blueprint of love, demonstrated
through the life and death of Jesus, the servant and Saviour:

> Greater love has no one than this, that someone lay
> down his life for his friends. You are my friends if you
> do what I command you.
> (John 15:13-14)

The ultimate demonstration of love was shown at Calvary
when Jesus laid down His life for every single one of us. We
are not being asked to die for someone, but the verse just
quoted provokes the thought. How much do we truly love?
How much are we willing to sacrifice for another person?

Would we give up our life – our plans, our family, our future – to save those same things for someone else?

In serving the Father, Jesus was willing to lay down His life for all mankind. His love was deep and unconditional, extending to every thief, every Barabbas, every Judas. This is what it means to look beyond the 'what'. Our service can often fall short because our compassion is limited to those we deem worthy of receiving it. If God had acted in that way, not one of us would be saved. As we serve Him, we are to follow the example of Jesus in the good that we do and the love that we show to everyone.

The act of doing good

Throughout the Old and New Testaments, our attention is drawn to the act of doing good. Here are some of those verses:

> Turn away from evil and do good;
> seek peace and pursue it.
> (Psalm 34:14)

> I have seen the business that God has given to the children of man to be busy with … I perceived that there is nothing better for them than to be joyful and to do good as long as they live.
> (Ecclesiastes 3:10, 12)

> Learn to do good;
> seek justice,
> correct oppression;
> bring justice to the fatherless,
> plead the widow's cause.
> (Isaiah 1:17)

> And let us not grow weary of doing good, for in due season we will reap, if we do not give up.
> (Galatians 6:9)

See that no one repays anyone evil for evil, but always
seek to do good to one another and to everyone.
(1 Thessalonians 5:15)

Do not neglect to do good and to share what you have,
for such sacrifices are pleasing to God.
(Hebrews 13:16)

It doesn't get much clearer than this, so let there be no doubt
that we are to pursue doing good. Maybe we have shied away
from 'the Lord's work' because it feels too big (I can't be a
missionary on the other side of the world), or too demanding
(I can't go into full-time ministry), or too hard (I don't have
the skills or resources). These misconceptions are based on
how this term is often used, but God's work is not
complicated or unachievable. Do we have the ability to do
good? Do we have the resources to be kind? Do we have a
heart to help others?

Let each of you look not only to his own interests, but
also to the interests of others.
(Philippians 2:4)

It is not usually a hard thing for any of us to show interest or
concern for someone else. Random acts of kindness happen
every day; big acts and small acts. It could be a phone call or
a card, a lift to church or the doctor's, walking the
neighbour's dog or simply helping someone to cross the road.
Something that seems small or insignificant to us can make
the world of difference to the person receiving it, so never
underestimate a small act of kindness. (Be open to the Holy
Spirit working within you, nudging you, directing you.) The
verse quoted above from Thessalonians says, 'always seek to
do good to one another and to everyone'. Those two words
'always seek' are an encouragement to actively look out for
the needs of others. We can ask God to open our eyes to

what those needs might be and then we listen for His guidance:

> Therefore ... be steadfast, immovable, always abounding in the work of the Lord, knowing that in the Lord your labour is not in vain.
> (1 Corinthians 15:58)

Service is the active part of our faith, and finding the Lord's work is a lot easier than we first may have thought. It is being aware of the challenges that others are facing, and offering practical help to make the situation a little easier. If we come across something that we can assist with, then we shouldn't hesitate to help, rather than falling into the trap of assuming that someone else will do what needs to be done. If God has opened our eyes to something, then we follow His direction.

There is so much need all around us and lots of people with serious struggles all trying to cope as best they can. We may not be able to address every difficulty, but we can draw alongside those who need a little support, and we can bring compassion and kindness to where it has not been before. Each one of us has good to do and the God-given ability to do it, so realistically, is there anything stopping us?

Work for everyone

As we saw at the start of the chapter, Jesus was not above practical service, and before He ascended back to heaven, we see Him once again in service to others.

Peter, Thomas, Nathanael and four of the other disciples had been out all night fishing, and Jesus knew that they hadn't caught a thing. They would be cold, tired, hungry and more than a little frustrated. Although just seeing Jesus would be enough to lift their spirits, the Lord was concerned about their whole well-being. Yes, He could simply speak to them and it would nourish their souls, but they were physically exhausted and Jesus cared about that too. So while He waited for them on the shore, He lit a fire and prepared breakfast for them.

Jesus had a wonderful way of illustrating spiritual things through practical actions. Having cooked the food and fed the disciples, Jesus turned to Peter and said, 'Feed my lambs' (John 21:15), and then again, 'Feed my sheep' (John 21:17). Jesus had supplied for Peter both spiritually and physically, and now He was handing over the reins. The directive for Peter was, 'Learn from Me and care for My flock,' which was summed up in the words, 'Follow me' (John 21:19), the same words He had used three years earlier. Peter could simply have accepted the Lord's will and work for his life and ended the conversation there, but curiosity got the better of him:

> Peter turned and saw the disciple whom Jesus loved
> following them ... [and] he said to Jesus, 'Lord, what
> about this man?'
> (John 21:20-21)

Peter had been given a work to do but he couldn't seem to help himself from wondering what John's role was going to be. Jesus did not indulge Peter's curiosity and basically told him not to concern himself about the work that John would be given.

We all have a role to play and work to do, and we should not be concerned as to whether the Lord has given someone else a 'better' task to do than us. First, we are all equal in the Father's eyes, and second, each role is uniquely tailored for each person's gifts.

When the Lord asks us to follow Him, He wants us to follow His lead and open ourselves up to the opportunities that He provides, using the talents and abilities He has blessed us with. Whatever the circumstances, God will never ask us to do anything for which He will not supply the strength, the power and the resources needed for it to be done. We will all have doubts regarding our own ability at times, which allows fear to creep in. Then, instead of responding like Samuel – 'Speak, for your servant hears' (1 Samuel 3:10) – we respond more like Moses – 'Oh, my Lord, please send someone else' (Exodus 4:13). When Moses thought of his own speaking ability in connection with God's task, he became paralysed with doubt and fear. Don't we all feel this way at times, believing we are inadequately equipped for the task ahead of us? Fear and doubt affect us all, and sometimes we hold on to that paralysis, not willing to believe it can change.

The first step in addressing our fear is to take God at His word:

> 'I say to you, rise, pick up your bed and go home.' And immediately he rose up before them and picked up what he had been lying on and went home, glorifying God.
> (Luke 5:24-25)

The paralysed man that Jesus was speaking to had legitimate reason to have fear and doubt. However, instead of exercising his fear, he chose to believe that the challenge was possible, so he exercised his faith and *immediately* rose up and walked home. Faith frees us from the paralysis of fear.

The Lord knows each of us intimately and He sees the great potential that we have when we walk with Him. When God says, 'Rise up,' He is saying, 'Rise up in My power and My strength, for My presence will go with you.' The best solution to fear and doubt is to trust God and have faith in His providence. When He calls, answer; where He leads, follow; then serve Him faithfully and confidently. Learn from the humble obedience of Jesus; always keep the towel and basin close at hand, and serve the Lord through works of compassion and kindness.

Tips for practical Christian service

I will show you my faith by my works.
(James 2:18)

If you want to be of real practical help and service, start making a list. Get to know your local area and the help that is currently available. For example:

- Where is the nearest food bank or community kitchen?

- Are there online activity or learning hubs for kids?

- Where are the mums-and-tots activities held?

- Are there winter warm spaces available?

- Does anywhere offer a lunch for seniors?

- Does the local care home have a pen-pal initiative?

- Do any of the local churches run a GriefShare[41] course?

- What are the helpline numbers for those struggling with drugs or alcohol?

- Are there counselling services in your area?

- Is there a Christians Against Poverty (CAP)[42] course being run anywhere?

This is not an exhaustive list; it is only a starting point. Build your own list, carry it with you and pray for God's guidance. This is great practical information to have, for it allows us to offer ideas and help to those who are experiencing difficult times.

---

[41] www.griefshare.org/ (accessed 16th April 2024).
[42] www.capuk.org (accessed 16th April 2024).

Practical Christianity is the combination of faith *and* works:

Faith – God is able to provide help in every situation.
Works – I am the help.

Reflections

Questions

- Do your thoughts on what 'the Lord's work' entails differ from previously, as a result of reading this chapter? How?

- Thinking about the story of the good Samaritan, how able are you to look beyond the 'what' to the 'who'?

- Have you heard God directing you towards a certain task but have allowed doubt or fear to creep in? How does God's Word help you to overcome your fear?

Practical application

Make a list of the help and services that are available in your local area and get to know the different community initiatives that are provided by the local churches. You might even find an area that you would like to get involved in.

Prayer

Father, I am thankful that when You send me out to do Your work, You send me out in Your strength. I ask that in all that I do, the power of the Spirit would continually stir up courage and grant me deeper access to the things of God. Increase my knowledge of You, Lord, so that I can serve with boldness and confidence, and face any opposition without fear. In Jesus' name. Amen.

11
Teaching us to pray: part one

Pray then like this:
'Our Father in heaven,
hallowed be your name.
Your kingdom come,
your will be done,
on earth as it is in heaven.'
(Matthew 6:9-10)

Prayer was essential to the Lord Jesus, and He was in the habit of rising early and going someplace quiet, often the mountainside, to talk to His Father. These conversations were vital to everything that the Lord would face and for what He was sent to accomplish. These were precious times of communion for seeking the will of His Father and the power of the Spirit for every aspect of the work ahead. As with all the lessons that Jesus taught, He led by example in how we should pray:

> When you pray, go into your room and shut the door
> and pray to your Father.
> (Matthew 6:6)

When it comes to personal prayer, Jesus gave us clear guidance in what to do and what not to do. This intimate communion should be reserved for a quiet place, away from the eyes of the world. It should be a time of honest reflection and not empty words. In saying, 'When you pray' (which we read three times in Matthew 6), Jesus was also letting us know that prayer is not an optional extra that we can take or leave; it is something that we are expected to do. Realistically, why wouldn't we? Prayer takes us into the throne room of Almighty God, granting us the privilege of speaking directly to the Father. This is our access point for seeking and receiving the guidance, strength, courage, patience and peace that we need to bolster our faith and see us through difficult and trying times. It is a place of bringing our praise and thankfulness for all that God has given, and it is where we intercede on behalf of others.

The prayer room is a wonderful place, and yet it is often neglected. Talking to Jesus/Father/Holy Spirit should be the most natural thing in the world. It should most definitely be a priority, and it is absolutely a necessity, so how do we improve our prayer life? How do we talk to God?

In this chapter we are going to look at the high priestly prayer of Jesus and listen to how He spoke to His Father. Through this prayer, we see not only the heart of a Saviour, but also the reality of who we are *in* Him, what we mean *to* Him and the hope that is ours *through* Him. You can read the full prayer in John 17, and I would encourage you to do that now.

The high priestly prayer

After the final Passover meal that was shared with the disciples, and before the betrayal by Judas, Jesus revealed to them the coming events in a little more detail. He would be leaving them soon, but He assured them that their sorrow would not last and that joy would return. He spoke of difficult times that would inevitably come, but reminded them of the wonderful truth that He had overcome all things. He did not want them to feel abandoned, and so He alleviated their fears with the promise of the Helper, who would lead them, guide them and help them remember all that He had told them.

Having told the disciples all that He needed to, Jesus lifted His eyes to heaven and prayed. It was a prayer that acknowledged the eternal plan and all those who have a place within it. It was a prayer for unity and protection for all who believe in Him; a prayer of intercession. Through it we can learn how to pray for one another and for the things that truly matter in our own lives. This incredible high priestly prayer is filled with pure love, deep concern and eternal hope.

Pure love

Jesus began His prayer with a solemn truth, 'Father, the hour has come' (John 17:1). We can feel the heaviness of His heart as He prepared for the fulfilment of His purpose, that through His death, eternal life would be made available to all. This was a dark time for Jesus, for the sin of the world – past, present and future – would be absorbed into His own body, and He would become the guilt offering for every single one of us.[43] Yet, knowing what was about to take place in the next few hours, He did not let His thoughts dwell there. His focus was lifted from Himself and directed towards all those He came to save. His focus was the eternal plan for eternal life, the plan that had been in motion from the very beginning. God desired a people who would live pure and holy lives, and who would commune with Him in holy worship. A people who would look after the wonderful world He had created, and on whom he could lavish every good thing... forever. The plan still exists and the choice to be a part of it is still available to whoever believes.

When we hear the Word of God and receive it as truth, believing that the Son of God came to earth as Christ the Saviour, we are changed by faith into a child of God and we

---

[43] See Isaiah 53.

now belong to Him. Identity secured. And just when you thought it couldn't get any better than *belonging* to Jesus, listen to what else He says:

> I am praying for them. I am not praying for the world but for those whom you have given me, for they are yours.
> (John 17:9)

If you have given your life to Jesus, He is praying for you. Really think about that for a minute – Jesus is praying for you! This is not a generic prayer for everyone on earth; it is specifically for all those who belong to Him and to the Father. Consider for a moment all those whom you lift up to God in prayer, and think about the love and concern that compels you to do that. Jesus loves us more deeply than we can even imagine, and He cares about every aspect of our lives. He is praying for our safety, our well-being, our spiritual growth. Every single thing about us matters because we are of great value to Him and He wants to protect us from the evils of this world.

Deep concern

Jesus came down to our world to open our eyes to the one responsible for its decay and destruction. He came down to dispel the darkness in which we walk, to show us the way out of the devil's deception and lead us into God's truth. He came down to make us aware of our sin, but then to assure us of the Father's steadfast love and to glorify the Father before all mankind.

The central part of Jesus' prayer conveys His deep concern for every one of His followers:

> I am no longer in the world, but they are in the world … I do not ask that you take them out of the world, but that you keep them from the evil one.
> (John 17:11, 15)

The precious souls that were entrusted into His care, He would no longer be with physically. Having accomplished the work He had been given to do, He was now returning home to the Father to undertake another kind of work: 'I go to prepare a place for you' (John 14:2). Jesus knew He must leave, and that His departure was necessary, but He wanted to make sure that those who belonged to Him would be looked after, so He prayed, 'Holy Father, keep them in your name' (John 17:11).

When we give our lives to God and become a part of His kingdom, this world becomes a foreign place, a place in which we no longer belong but a place in which we must live. We are very much like Daniel in captivity in Babylon – a foreign country with its own social norms and practices, with a people who worship their own gods and idols – and it can sometimes feel like we are standing in a den of lions. Jesus understands the reality of what that means, which is why He lifted us up before the Father and said, 'For their sake I consecrate myself, that they also may be sanctified in truth' (John 17:19). Jesus consecrated Himself in holy service for our sake and He prayed that the Father would keep us from the lies of the devil and the jaws of evil, in order that we would remain holy as we live in this world:

> As you sent me into the world, so I have sent them into the world.
> (John 17:18)

When Jesus prayed this beautiful priestly prayer to the Father, He referred to His followers as 'the people whom you gave me out of the world' (John 17:6), so we belong to Him first and foremost. This prayer gives us a glimpse of our Lord's heart and of the deep concern that He has for each one of us. Jesus knew what a hard and difficult place the world could be. He had been hated and He knew that society's contempt for truth would be passed on to all His followers. So, with all the understanding of what we would face in this world, Jesus gave Himself wholly over to the Father that we might be divinely blessed in truth and purified by the Word.

In this pure state, Jesus releases us back into the battle to spread His life-changing gospel. He doesn't want us to hide away behind closed doors; He wants us out, telling the truth of who He is. He doesn't want us following the crowd; He wants us leading it. Forget the idea of trying to quietly fit in and not make waves; Jesus wants us to rock the boat! He has sent us back into the world to change it, not conform to it, which irritates the devil no end, and he will try everything to block our attempts to implement God's truth.

Spiritual warfare is real, and the prince of this world will try to cause havoc for every believer. As we pray, we need to ask the Lord for His continued protection, not only over our own lives and the lives of those we love, but also over every brother and sister in Christ. We glorify the Lord Jesus by standing strong and firm together, in the truth of God's Word. We are in the world, but, more importantly, we are in the Father and we are kept secure in the power of His name.

Eternal hope

And this is eternal life, that they know you the only true God, and Jesus Christ whom you have sent.
(John 17:3)

Jesus was the redemptive plan for the eternal plan. Having achieved all that had been asked of Him, He declared, 'I glorified you on earth, having accomplished the work that you gave me to do' (John 17:4). Jesus completed the personal work He had been charged with, which is why He could definitively say, 'It is finished' (John 19:30).

If you haven't yet discovered your own personal work, then pray that God would reveal it to you. If you are doing His work, then pray that you would be faithful in completing it. It would be such a wonderful thing to be able to say at the end of our time here, 'I glorified You on earth, having accomplished the work that You gave me.'

Alongside our personal work, we also have a collective work to do as the salt of the earth and the light of the world. As we pray for one another and fulfil this calling, we bring glory to the One in whom we belong.

Everyone has a need to belong because it is where we find our identity. In joining groups or organisations of like-minded people, there is a sense of finding value and worth as well as feeling that we belong to *something*. Of all the things and places that I have belonged to over the years, the one that has given me my true identity is in belonging to Jesus.

So how are we sure that we belong to Him? Quite simply because He said so:

> All mine are yours, and yours are mine, and I am glorified in them.
> (John 17:10)

Perfect unity

The Lord's desire was that every believer would be united together in Him. He wanted unity and a oneness among His people, Jew and Gentile alike, as He said in His teaching, 'I have other sheep that are not of this fold [the house of Israel]. I must bring them also, and they will listen to my voice. So there will be one flock, one shepherd' (John 10:16).

The union of the Trinity has a power like no other and a strength that nothing can break. Jesus wants that same power and strength for His people. The importance of it is such that He mentions being 'one' four times in His prayer. The Lord wants us united because, 'though a man might prevail against one who is alone, two will withstand him [and] a threefold cord is not quickly broken' (Ecclesiastes 4:12). Jesus knows how much stronger we are together than apart, and for this unity He passes on to us the glory that He received from the Father:

> The glory that you have given me I have given to them, that they may be one even as we are one, I in them and you in me, that they may become perfectly one, so that the world may know that you sent me and loved them even as you loved me.
> (John 17:22-23)

Division weakens the message of the gospel, but perfect unity in Christ enables us to demonstrate the perfect love of the Father which brings healing to all who are broken. Our prayers should include this twofold desire for unity. First, that our personal union with God would be continually strengthened – spirit to Spirit. Second, that we would strive towards the collective union of the Church of Jesus Christ – the bride of the Bridegroom:

> Father, I desire that they also, whom you have given me, may be with me where I am.
> (John 17:24)

The Father gave us (the Church) to the Son as His bride, and the Bridegroom longs for our presence with Him. How beautiful is that thought! Do you desire to be with the Lord? Does it surprise you to know that His desire is to be with you? It is individuals that make up the collective Church, so this prayer is personal. Jesus offers up these heartfelt words because He loves you; He is praying for your protection because you belong to Him. His ultimate desire, however, is to have you with Him in heaven. Until that day arrives, we continue to serve Him, individually and collectively, in the knowledge of His deep and profound love, which surrounds us every day of our journey here on earth. This prayer assures us that we do not walk this narrow path alone, for we are kept in the hands of the Father and in the heart of Jesus our Lord. His concern for us is ongoing and He never stops providing all that we need as we live for Him:

> I made known to them your name, and I will continue
> to make it known, that the love with which you have
> loved me may be in them, and I in them.
> (John 17:26)

Not only is the Father revealed to us as the God of our salvation, but He is continually being made known to us, to the fullness of who He is. This knowledge grants us a deeper understanding of the One we love and serve, and guides us into a deeper relationship with Father, Son and Holy Spirit. Knowing who God is enables us to lift our eyes as Jesus did, and say in reverent truth, 'Our Father in heaven, hallowed be your name' (Matthew 6:9).

Reflections

Questions

- How is prayer-time for you – have you found it to be a priority, a necessity or an afterthought? Is your prayer life changing? In what way?

- As you consider the high priestly prayer, how do you feel about the pure love, the deep concern and the eternal hope that Jesus expresses?

- Jesus prays for you. How does that truth impact your sense of security and identity?

Practical application

Choose to make prayer a priority this week. When I wake up each day, I say, 'Good morning, Lord, thank You for another day; help me use it wisely.' If this is something that you have never done or rarely do, I encourage you to give it a go. The best start to any day is in connecting to God.

Prayer

Lord Jesus, my mind cannot fully comprehend the depth of Your love for me or the amazing truth that You pray for me, but I am incredibly thankful and humbled that You do. I know that whatever comes my way, You are standing by my side and interceding on my behalf. Keep me, Lord, from the lies of the devil and help me to remain focused on Your truth, so that I would walk faithfully with You. Amen.

12

Teaching us to pray: part two

Ask, and it will be given to you; seek, and you will find;
knock, and it will be opened to you.
(Matthew 7:7)

The essential habit of prayer

The conversations that Jesus had with the Father were vital for everything that He would face and for all that He was sent to accomplish. Likewise, prayer is essential for our daily lives and all that they entail. We too need these precious times of communion to seek the power and strength of the Spirit in order to carry out the plan and purpose of God in every aspect of our lives. If we only come to Him in times of emergency, then we are missing out on so much. Prayer is a two-way conversation, not a one-way monologue from earth to heaven.

Most of us have probably had a message from a friend asking, 'Do you want to meet for a coffee?' We choose the place and the time and then look forward to the catch-up. Somehow, time with a friend always seems to fly by as the conversation flows. It's easy conversation; it's comfortable and relaxing, for there is no need for pretence – we can just 'be'.

This is the kind of conversation that God wants to have with us. He wants to meet with us on a regular basis. He wants us to discover that talking to Him can feel like the most natural thing in the world. We can bring our joys, our fears, our achievements and our failures. We don't have to hide anything from Him. We can be open; we can be honest; we can just 'be'. In order to grow in faith, we need to talk and listen to God. In finding our purpose, we need to talk and listen to God. To be able to serve efficiently, we need to talk and listen to God. To walk this narrow path and come through the battles – well, you get the picture.

Prayer in challenging times

Prayer is essential, especially for the battles, for we don't demonstrate our faith through the easy times; we demonstrate our faith through the hard and challenging times. One of the challenges that comes to each of us is when someone hurts us, betrays us or wrongs us in some way. What can be even more challenging is when the wrong is done to someone we love:

> Love your enemies and pray for those who persecute you.
> (Matthew 5:44)

This is not an easy verse, but then, if we only live our Christian life through the verses we like, can we honestly say we are walking in the fullness of Christ? Challenging times will come to everyone's door, and we will all react to them in different ways. Talking to God about these situations may not be the first thing on our list, but eventually we should bring our anger, our hurt and our tears to God.

When the challenge of hurt and betrayal came to my door and I cried out in frustration to God, I wanted Him to right the wrong, and I wanted to be vindicated in my anger. God, however, does not look at things the same way I do, and instead of handing out divine retribution, He gave a command – pray for the one who has caused you distress.

Pray for them? Really? I don't want to pray for them, I want to tell everyone what kind of person they really are! I want everyone to know what they did! I certainly don't want to show them love. Yet that is exactly what God wants and expects of me if I am living in the attitude of Christ.

The Lord Jesus chose to love us even though we sinned (and continue to sin) against Him. He granted us mercy; He poured out His grace and He forgave us. He prayed for His enemies and for those who persecuted Him:

> But where sin increased, grace abounded all the more.
> (Romans 5:20)

It is not an easy thing to pray for someone who has caused you hurt or pain; being completely honest, it is something that I struggled with for years. The first time you do it, and possibly the hundredth time you do it, it will feel extremely uncomfortable. It may take a long time to turn anger into grace, but when we keep praying, we will feel the shift in our spirit and in our heart. Prayer may not always change the person being prayed for, but it will most definitely change the person who is praying. Prayer guides us through the darkness of hurt and along the cliff edge of betrayal until it brings us to the path of healing. The truly wonderful thing is that while we are praying for someone else, Jesus is praying for us. Remember what He said to Peter:

> I have prayed for you that your faith may not fail. And when you have turned again, strengthen your brothers.
> (Luke 22:32)

Following God's commands can be more difficult than we like to admit at times. My prayer walk of forgiveness felt like I was walking on shards of glass, and the cuts refused to heal. The longer the situation went on, the worse I felt, because I wasn't just holding on to my anger, I was also failing to trust

God's direction. Failure feels horrible and I had apologised to God so many times that I was sure His patience was running out.

Thankfully, in His grace, the Father never views our failure as a barrier to success, but more of a wrong turn that needs correcting. Another great example of this is Jonah, who was given clear directions from God but failed to follow them. He didn't so much take a wrong turn, though, as purposely run in the other direction, but instead of ending on that failure, God said, 'OK, let's try this again.'

There are so many characters in the Bible who struggled in their walk with God, and yet the Lord continued to use them and guide them and bless them. Failure is by no means the end of the journey; it is the crossroads where God's grace is waiting to strengthen us once more. Jonah found that strength, as did Peter, as did I, and we were each able to 'turn again' and follow the Lord's commands.

Failure is not to be feared. We confront it, accept it and let God use our experience to strengthen others. When the challenge comes, we allow the Spirit of God to help us move forward in grace, instead of anger or despair. Then we put our trust in a Sovereign God and trust the power of persistent prayer to bring about change.

Pray without ceasing

To 'pray without ceasing' (1 Thessalonians 5:17) sounds like a very tall order and, realistically, unachievable, but if we are being asked to do it, then it must be doable. So what does 'without ceasing' really mean? The Greek word used for this is *adialeiptōs*, which is defined as uninterrupted, to the extent that it is continually recurring.

There are different types of prayer. For example, there are prayers of praise, prayers of thanksgiving and prayers of intercession, but the prayer we tend to use the most is the prayer for change. These prayers contain our wishes and desires, and all those things we long to see happen; the things that need changing from how they presently are. These are not one-off prayers; these are the prayers that are recurring. To 'pray without ceasing' means bringing a request before God over and over again. Continual prayer is persistent prayer.

We know that prayer was important to the Lord Jesus, and it was something that He wanted His followers to understand. To aid in this, He chose a parable of an unrighteous judge and a widow to show how we benefit when we pray without ceasing:

> In a certain city there was a judge who neither feared God nor respected man. And there was a widow in that city who kept coming to him and saying, 'Give me justice against my adversary.'
> (Luke 18:2-3)

In this parable, Jesus told the story of a man with power, authority and great responsibility. Unfortunately, he was so full of his own importance that he cared little for anything else. He was a judge who did not fear any higher power, and those he deemed lower than him received no respect. When a widow came to him for help, asking for justice against her adversary, he said no. When she came back a second time asking for justice, he again said no, but she was not deterred. Her need was so great that she was unwilling to give up. She came back again and again, not put off by his refusal to help. She persisted continually until the judge said to himself, 'Because this widow keeps bothering me, I will give her justice, so that she will not beat me down by her continual coming' (Luke 18:5). Persistence, in the end, paid off.

Jesus pointed out to His listeners that this unrighteous man eventually did what was right for the widow who came to him. So if an unrighteous judge can do what is right, how much more will the Righteous Judge do right:

> Will not God give justice to his elect, who cry to him
> day and night? Will he delay long over them? I tell you,
> he will give justice to them speedily.
> (Luke 18:7-8)

The lesson Jesus wants us to learn is not to lose heart in prayer, but to 'pray without ceasing' and never lose faith in what God can do. He challenges us to do this with His final question: 'When the Son of Man comes, will he find faith on earth?' (Luke 18:8). God's love and compassion for us never wane; every time we cry out to Him, He hears and He will answer. Patience and persistence are the twins of prayer, and exercising both of them means never giving up on the power of God to change the unchangeable.

Always choose prayer

Whatever is going on in our life, we should bring every part of it to God on a regular basis. In following the example and teaching of Jesus in addressing God as Father, we acknowledge the privileged relationship that we have with Him:

> Because you are sons [and daughters], God has sent
> the Spirit of his Son into our hearts, crying, 'Abba!
> Father!'
> (Galatians 4:6)

In calling God 'Father', we are securing our identity in Him within our own spirit. We belong to Almighty God, the One who reigns with sovereignty over all things. There is nothing that takes place without His knowledge, and everything is under His control. For this reason, we hand every single aspect of our lives over to Him, saying, 'Your will be done' (Matthew 6:10). Our heavenly Father knows all that we are dealing with day to day and all that we have yet to face.

As we make prayer an essential habit and chat to God throughout the day, we don't need to leave anything out or ever think that something is too trivial to bring before Him. We can just be ourselves in His presence, for we never have to pretend to be anything else. As we pray, we trust in the One who is able to keep us from falling, the One who guards and protects us, the One for whom we have been set apart and to whose kingdom we belong.

Prayer strengthens our relationship with the Father, the Son and the Holy Spirit; this is the strength that we need for every challenge that comes our way. It is the strength we need for the onward journey along the narrow path.

Reflections

Questions

- When you think about the idea of having a conversation with God (as opposed to a one-way monologue), does it feel natural, or uncomfortable, or weird, or (something else)? Spend time thinking about this.

- God can use our 'wrong turn' experiences to help others come through similar situations. In what ways might God do this in your own life?

- Consider the situations that you pray for over and over again – why do you think you might give up praying in one scenario and yet be compelled to pray without ceasing in another?

Practical application

Think back over the last seven days – things that have happened, people you've spoken to, situations that have challenged or moved you. Choose something for each of the four prayer types – praise, thanksgiving, intercession, change. Write in your notebook the 'who', the 'what' or the 'why' for each one. Think about developing this into a good habit.

Prayer

Father, I know that conversation is vital to growing a relationship, and I am sorry that I don't talk to You as often as I should. I know that I can bring everything and anything to You in prayer – no matter how big or how small. Help me, Lord, to develop a natural prayer life in which talking to You becomes second nature. Thank You for Your patience and Your grace. Amen.

13
Lessons for the journey

Everyone who comes to me and hears my words and does them, I will show you what he is like: he is like a man building a house, who dug deep and laid the foundation on the rock. And when a flood arose, the stream broke against that house and could not shake it, because it had been well built.
(Luke 6:47-48)

In the introduction to this book, I said that the lessons of Jesus are forthright, challenging and often tough, but what they produce is a deep-rooted life of faith which stands on a solid foundation. Christ is our cornerstone, [44] and every lesson that He gives helps us to build a strong and steadfast faith. In Luke 6, Jesus emphasises the importance of building on a firm substructure, and compares those who do with those who don't. These two groups of builders hear the same lessons that Jesus is teaching, but the outcomes are poles apart. One group hears what is said and does what Jesus taught; the other group hears the lessons but disregards them as unimportant.

When we accept the truth of Jesus' teaching and choose to build our lives on His principles, He becomes the bedrock

---

[44] Ephesians 2:20; 1 Peter 2:6-7.

of our faith. When the rains come and the challenges of life bombard us like a surging river, that faith remains unshaken. In anchoring ourselves to Christ and living our lives in obedience to Him, our foundation remains secure. Conversely, those who hear but dismiss the teaching of Jesus are 'like a man who built a house on the ground without a foundation. When the stream broke against it, immediately it fell, and the ruin of that house was great' (Luke 6:49). In this scenario there is no foundation, and that is where we find the key to this whole analogy – obedience to God's Word: 'Everyone who ... hears my words and does them' (Luke 6:47).

These two houses may look the same from the outside, but the builders used different blueprints. One chose a self-build design with a sub-base of self-righteousness, while the other chose 'the righteousness of God through faith in Jesus Christ' (Romans 3:22):

> By wisdom a house is built,
> and by understanding it is established.
> (Proverbs 24:3)

Just like the lessons of Jesus, the onward journey for the Christian will be challenging, which is why the foundation of our faith is crucial and the understanding of it is vital. Each one of us needs to know what we believe and why we believe it. We need to understand the cost, the commitment and the continual process of establishing a deep-rooted faith. We need a clear understanding of who we are in Christ and our place in the kingdom of God. We need an awareness of our purpose here on earth, as well as an appreciation of the effect that our attitude and behaviour can have on those around us. We need to develop a heart of service and understand the importance of daily conversations with God.

Having a concrete understanding of our faith, through the lessons that Jesus taught, gives us the ability to be salt and light, to be wheat among weeds and lambs among wolves:

> Go your way; behold, I am sending you out as lambs
> in the midst of wolves.
> (Luke 10:3)

At first glance, this may not be one of the most encouraging statements in terms of who we are, but it is much less daunting when we truly understand who it is that sends us out. As we go and spread the truth of the gospel through our everyday lives, Jesus is with us. In the same way that some accepted the words of Jesus and others rejected them, we too will have similar experiences. There will be those who accept what they hear and receive Jesus as Lord and Saviour, and those who will reject the truth as irrelevant to their situation. Jesus said:

> The one who hears you hears me, and the one who
> rejects you rejects me, and the one who rejects me
> rejects him who sent me.
> (Luke 10:16)

The scene in Luke 10 is of Jesus sending out seventy-two of His disciples (lambs) into somewhat hostile territory (wolves), yet we read that they returned with joy, saying, 'Lord, even the demons are subject to us in your name!' (Luke 10:17). These disciples had watched Jesus heal the lame, the blind, the diseased; they had seen Him raise the dead and cast out demons. He had a power and authority that knew no bounds, and He had given it to them. Imagine how they must have felt the first time they experienced that power working through them. It's no wonder they returned with such excitement and were, no doubt, pleased with what they had achieved. However, Jesus did the work of the Father with humility, and He wanted His disciples to appreciate the authority they had been given without gloating about it. He confirmed to them that, yes, He had indeed given them power, but 'Nevertheless, do not rejoice in this... but rejoice that your names are written in heaven' (Luke 10:20). Jesus wanted them to understand that it was not about what they could do but about who they were – sons of the kingdom, sent out to bring others in.

Jesus continues to send His disciples out today and we are still lambs among wolves, but we have no reason to fear, for we are sons and daughters of the King and His power always dwells within us. We can walk through the hostile territory, face the tough challenges and ride out any storm that comes our way, because in His power we can emerge victorious!

Navigating rough waters

Have you ever been on a boat in very stormy weather? It's not much fun; in fact, it can be quite frightening, even for seasoned sailors. For the twelve disciples, travelling with Jesus meant numerous boat trips across the Sea of Galilee. One reason for this would obviously be time, as it would be quicker to sail across the lake than to walk around it. Walking also meant having crowds on your heels continually, while a boat trip meant that Jesus could take some rest between teaching.

This is exactly what Jesus was doing on one particular trip when a severe windstorm made sailing hazardous. The fishermen among the twelve would have been used to rough waters, but the others were much more accustomed to solid ground, and right now that ground was waterlogged and tilting back and forth. Stress levels began rising with every wave:

> A great windstorm arose, and the waves were breaking into the boat, so that the boat was already filling. But he [Jesus] was in the stern, asleep on the cushion.
> (Mark 4:37-38)

Can we really blame them for being a bit anxious about the storm and bewildered that Jesus was sleeping through it? A question I have asked myself is whether I would have wakened Jesus or just tried to shelter as close to Him as possible. After all, He didn't seem to be at all concerned. Fear, however, took hold of the disciples and they woke Jesus from His sleep, asking, 'Teacher, do you not care that we are perishing?' (Mark 4:38).

Each of us may have asked God this question, in one form or another, when going through our own storm; those times in life when circumstances seem overwhelming, the outcome seems bleak and we don't know which way to turn. During those times, it is not unusual to be anxious and to cry out to God, wondering if He can see what's happening and asking whether He cares or not. Sometimes it is only when the storm passes that we realise He was right there with us in the boat the whole time.

Having been wakened from His rest, Jesus said to the twelve, 'Where is your faith?' (Luke 8:25). This might seem like a strange question at first for Jesus to ask. Did He mean that the boat was strong enough to weather the storm, so they should have had faith in the vessel? Doubtful. Did He mean that they should have had faith in their own ability to see the storm through? Definitely not. So what, then? What faith did they need? The answer is found at the start of the story:

> One day he [Jesus] got into a boat with his disciples, and he said to them, 'Let us go across to the other side of the lake.'
> (Luke 8:22)

Did you see it? First, the most obvious thing is that Jesus got into the boat *with* them. Whatever was going to happen, He would be right beside them through it all. Second, Jesus intended for them to reach the planned destination: 'Let *us* go' (my emphasis). The faith that Jesus was looking for in the disciples was their faith in Him. Not in the boat and not in themselves, but absolute faith in Him and His Word.

We can trust God in every situation, because His Word and His promises are true:

171

> It is the LORD who goes before you. He will be with you; he will not leave you or forsake you. Do not fear or be dismayed.
> (Deuteronomy 31:8)

Life will get messy and challenging, but just as Jesus spoke peace into the storm, He can speak peace into our very being and grant us grace to ride out the storm: 'My grace is sufficient for you, for my power is made perfect in weakness' (2 Corinthians 12:9). This is what the Lord said to the apostle Paul when his circumstances became challenging.

Sometimes the situation does not change the way we want it to (it didn't for Paul), which can be really hard for us to accept at times. Don't mistake this for God not caring; He doesn't enjoy seeing His children suffer. Imagine any parent with a sick child and the lengths they go to in supporting them through the situation. They constantly reassure their child that whatever happens, they won't have to go through it alone; they (the parent) will be beside them through the whole experience. This is our God, walking beside us for the whole journey, pouring His grace continually upon us. He is steadfast and sure in every storm.

We do not deserve God's favour but He gives it generously because His compassion towards us knows no limit, and neither does His faithfulness. Relying on God's grace alone in difficult times is not easy, but if we allow it, it will bring peace.

In Acts 11, Barnabas rejoiced in the grace that God had given to the believers at Antioch, encouraging them to stay faithful to God and to persevere. Likewise, our circumstances should never change our faithfulness to God, because they can never change who we are in Him. We are His children and He is with us through every situation. Paul did not rely on his own power to change his circumstances, and the disciples did not rely on their own power to battle the storm. We, therefore, should not rely on our own strength, whatever the challenge, but say, like Paul, 'I will boast all the more gladly of my weaknesses, so that the power of Christ may rest upon me' (2 Corinthians 12:9).

Another wonderful truth about our God is that he does not 'slumber nor sleep' (Psalm 121:4), so we don't need to wake Him and alert Him to our situation. He sees every detail of our lives: 'For the eyes of the LORD run to and fro throughout the whole earth, to give strong support to those whose heart is blameless towards him' (2 Chronicles 16:9). Our heavenly Father knows all our circumstances fully, and He cares for us more deeply than we could ever imagine. So, whenever we feel the pressure to ask the question, 'Lord, do you not care that I am drowning?', remember, He is always working things out for our good,[45] and there is no situation that He cannot work through. The Lord understands the turmoil and tragedy that we endure; He knows every trial and every sorrow we will face within this broken world. The difficult times are very real, but so is His presence. Whatever life throws at us, we can confidently hand everything over to God and trust that His presence with us ensures that His planned destination for us will be reached.

Instructions to follow

We have established that the journey through life is far from easy because life is never straightforward, but we have also discovered that Jesus is our steadfast companion, every step of the way. He is the light that guides us, the spiritual bread that feeds us and the Shepherd that goes before us. He is our way through directionless wanderings; our truth in a world of deception; our source of life, of joy and of peace. His Word brings us encouragement, comfort, strength, guidance and wisdom as well as containing instructions to follow for walking this narrow path:

---

[45] Romans 8:28.

> Ask, and it will be given to you; seek, and you will find;
> knock, and it will be opened to you.
> (Matthew 7:7)

The apostle Paul tells us that God's Word is:

> profitable for teaching, for reproof, for correction,
> and for training in righteousness, that the man of God
> may be competent, equipped for every good work.
> (2 Timothy 3:16-17)

Within the context of teaching, the Bible is our handbook for daily living. That being said, it doesn't list every single situation that we will find ourselves in. There isn't a chapter and verse that we can look up which addresses specifics such as buying a new car, which house to rent, starting a business, etc. This is where Matthew 7:7 comes in. Jesus is highlighting the importance of communication with the Father. He is saying that if you are struggling with something or unsure about anything, then ask God about it, seek out the answer and allow the door of heaven to open up the way.

Jesus wants His followers to rely on His guidance for every situation that life presents. He wants us to ask how to deal with difficult interactions, to seek His approach in handling conflict and to pursue the Father's will in all things, all of the time. Whatever a day may bring, we take it to God and ask Him to help us find the right answer, the right approach and the right attitude for all that we face. We serve a generous God who wants to give good gifts to all His sons and daughters. He does not skimp on goodness and there is no limit on His giving, for there is no limit to His love for us:

> As the Father has loved me, so have I loved you.
> Abide in my love.
> (John 15:9)

This limitless love, flowing down from the Father, is where Jesus wants us to stay. That is what the word 'abide' means – to continue; stay; dwell; remain. Everything we need comes from the Lord. He is pure love. If we remain in Him then His love will continually flow down through us, filling us, saturating us. From that, the fruit of the Spirit[46] will become evident in our lives. A plant or tree that is rooted in perfect soil, getting the sun and the rain, cannot help but produce flowers or berries or food. That is us, rooted in the Word of God, in the love of the Lord Jesus and in the sustaining power of the Holy Spirit.

When we choose to remain in the love of Jesus and follow His teachings, our lives will bear fruit for Him. Jesus said, 'By this my Father is glorified, that you bear much fruit and so prove to be my disciples' (John 15:8). The Holy Spirit helps us to grow in knowledge and understanding of the gospel of Christ, and brings to memory all that we have learned. As we put those lessons into practice, we will start to produce the good fruit that brings glory to God. Every day we have the opportunity to live productive lives for Jesus. We won't always get it right and we will have our stumbles along the way, but the wonderful thing about our God is that His mercies 'are new every morning' (Lamentations 3:22-23). We don't let a bad day knock us off track; we dust ourselves off, talk to God about what went wrong and receive His forgiveness. There is a lot of work to be done for the kingdom, and the last thing that the devil wants is for us to be doing a good job. We need to be vigilant for his distractions and pitfalls, recognising them for what they are when they come.

Our focus should always be Jesus, for He will always show us the way. He came to lead us back to the Father and He paved the path that would lead us home. His time of teaching may have been short, but it was perfectly packed with the

---

[46] Galatians 5:22-23.

truth, wisdom and understanding that we would need for the journey. He left us in the safekeeping of the Father and the presence of the Spirit. He also left us with the expectation that He would one day come back to take home all those who have believed and trusted in Him. In the anticipation of His return, we are given this instruction:

> Stay dressed for action and keep your lamps burning ... be ready, for the Son of Man is coming at an hour you do not expect.
> (Luke 12:35, 40)

When Jesus returns, it will be sudden and without warning, so making sure we are prepared is paramount. On that day there will be no second chances, for Jesus said, 'Two men will be in the field; one will be taken and one left. Two women will be grinding at the mill; one will be taken and one left' (Matthew 24:40-41). He explained the reality of that day further through the story of the ten virgins, of whom five were wise and five were foolish. They all went out to meet the bridegroom although they didn't know the time of his arrival. All of them took their lamps, but only the wise brought extra oil; only the wise were prepared. 'The bridegroom came, and those who were ready went in with him to the marriage feast, and the door was shut' (Matthew 25:10).

The lesson in this is for us not to become complacent as we live in the anticipation of Christ's return. If we knew that the Lord was coming back next week, would it create more of an urgency to talk to family and friends who have not yet accepted Christ as their Saviour? Would our service to God be stagnant, or our purpose put on hold? We have a tendency to live with the notion of having plenty of time, but what if there is not as much of it as we think?

Jesus told His disciples that before He would return, the earth would see 'great distress' (Luke 21:23). He had a pressing need to prepare them for all that would come, yet at the same time to encourage them to continue the work, no matter what. By knowing what was to come, they (and we) could be properly equipped for the battle, both spiritually and mentally. In Luke 21 we hear Jesus explain the distress that will be seen across the world and the fear that will come upon it, 'for the powers of the heavens will be shaken' (v26). When we watch the news and see moral decline in all its horrific guises, how many times have we said, or heard someone say, 'What is the world coming to?' As the Church gets squeezed out or, worse still, conforms to society, the world slowly decays and it appears that the devil has the upper hand. Against this, Jesus says:

> Watch yourselves lest your hearts be weighed down with dissipation and ... cares of this life ... Stay awake at all times, praying that you may have strength to escape all these things that are going to take place.
> (Luke 21:34, 36)

> The Son of Man [is] coming in a cloud with power and great glory ... [so] straighten up and raise your heads, because your redemption is drawing near.
> (Luke 21:27-28)

Jesus never hid the fact that we would encounter difficulties in this life on earth, as well as see distress all across the world. He knows that alongside all that is good, we will endure real frustration, real pain and real sorrow. He instructs us to be mindful of it and not to let it overtake us. When we feel the weight of life becoming heavy to bear, we raise our heads, for His strength is real; we straighten up, for His grace is real; we praise His Name, for our redemption is real.

When we trust in all that Jesus has taught us, we can move forward with confidence and boldness, in the power of the Spirit.

Reflections

Questions

- What type of foundation are you building your faith upon?

- What frightens you about being a light in the dark, wheat among weeds or a lamb among wolves? What is it, for you, that takes this fear away?

- How confident are you that God will help you to find the right answer, the right approach and the right attitude for all that you will face on this journey? What are you basing that confidence on?

Practical application
Spend some time memorising Luke 6:47-48:

> Everyone who comes to me and hears my words and does them, I will show you what he is like: he is like a man building a house, who dug deep and laid the foundation on the rock. And when a flood arose, the stream broke against that house and could not shake it, because it had been well built.

Prayer
Thank You, Jesus, for being the sure foundation of my life. I know that when the rains come, I can stand firm because I am anchored to You. Help me, Lord, to continue to build wisely, with every brick connected to the truth of Your Word. Help me to trust You in every storm. Let me always be aware of Your presence and never doubt that You are right there beside me through it all. In Your precious name I pray. Amen.

14
Moving forward in faith

I have been crucified with Christ. It is no longer I who live, but Christ who lives in me. And the life I now live in the flesh I live by faith in the Son of God, who loved me and gave himself for me.
(Galatians 2:20)

Most Christians that I have talked to have verses that they go to time and time again. It may be a verse that brings comfort or strength in difficult days, or a verse that brings joy and literally makes the heart sing. The verse above provides real encouragement, and it has always given me strength and courage to face any circumstance, knowing that Christ lives within me.

However, when I read this verse again recently, something had shifted and I experienced a feeling of shame alongside a sense of awe. I wondered if I could really say with confidence, 'It is no longer I who live.' In the last couple of years, I have been a lot more mindful of how weak the flesh (my own will) truly is and how much of a hindrance it is to the spiritual will. I refer to my own will as my sin-shell and it is a constant weakness that I cannot shed. Awareness of my continued sin was leading me into feelings of guilt, because Christ living in me means that He is carrying my sin on a daily basis. My own thoughts were taking me captive when I should have been living free. I needed to take my freedom back and walk in the truth of this verse once more; I needed to walk in the Spirit. God's life-giving Word reminded me that 'the law of the Spirit of life has set you free in Christ Jesus from the law of sin and death' (Romans 8:2). It also brought me to this promise of God which says, 'I will be merciful towards their iniquities, and I will remember their sins no more' (Hebrews 8:12). Jesus has taken all of my shame and guilt – past, present and future – paid for it with His own blood and then removed it from His remembrance forever. Because of this glorious truth, I live free.

We all have the opportunity to live in the freedom of Galatians 2:20. Confessing sin the moment it occurs helps to keep it from taking hold and helps us recognise the work of the Spirit in strengthening the faith by which we live:

> Repent therefore, and turn again, that your sins may be blotted out, that times of refreshing may come from the presence of the Lord.
> (Acts 3:19-20)

Turning from sin should not just apply to those who have not yet accepted Christ as Saviour. For the Christian, keeping our sin in check should be part of our everyday routine, asking God to make us aware of when we stray from the path. We can easily fall into the trap of thinking we are doing OK and not acknowledging the little slips along the way. Not all sin is immediately obvious, so it is good practice to take stock, from time to time, of what our day and week entails. I have to ask myself if I am using 'God time' for some other activity. Has what started out as an hour a day of meditation with the Lord slowly become forty-five minutes, thirty minutes, fifteen? Even if what I am doing is good, if it is replacing time with the Lord then it is hindering my relationship with Him. I need to 'repent therefore, and turn again', immersing myself in His presence.

Sin takes up space where peace should be; that is why it is so important to rest, reflect, receive God's forgiveness and find restoration in the presence of the Lord: 'Learn from me, for I am gentle and lowly in heart, and you will find rest for your souls' (Matthew 11:29). We learn from Jesus by following His lead. He continually stepped away from the busyness of life in order to spend time with the Father, a time of refreshing for His spirit. 'Times of refreshing' are essential for us also, and the presence of the Lord is the greatest resource we have for that to happen. In His presence we find our strength.

The good fight of faith

The resources of the Lord are vital in keeping and sustaining us for all that lies ahead. We will never be able to avoid sin completely while living in this world, but we can arm ourselves against it as much as possible. God has provided us with the armour we need for the everyday battlefield. It is a spiritual battle that rages on continually, whether we always recognise it or not, 'For we do not wrestle against flesh and blood' (Ephesians 6:12).

For a soldier to step out onto a battlefield without the proper protection would be dire, and yet the Christian so often steps out into the world every day without the full armour of God. We talk quite a lot about having, and relying on, the strength of the Lord, and we know that we need it, but how many mornings do we dive straight into the day without asking for it? The moment we head out unarmed, the devil swings into action. His aim? To shake our faith and weaken us in any way He can. But when we go out armed, we have power to overcome the ploys of the devil.[47]

Each day we need to take up the whole armour of God, as mentioned in Ephesians 6:10-18 – the belt of truth, the breastplate of righteousness, the shoes of the readiness to

[47] Ephesians 6:11.

share the gospel of peace, the shield of faith, the helmet of salvation and the sword of the Spirit. God's armour enables us to stand ready and stand firm with confidence, because we stand in the strength of *his* might:

> Fear not, for I am with you;
> be not dismayed, for I am your God;
> I will strengthen you, I will help you,
> I will uphold you with my righteous right hand.
> (Isaiah 41:10)

The Lord does not want us to only rely on Him when things are tough, He wants us to rely on Him for every single aspect of our day. 'In all circumstances' we are to 'take up the shield of faith' (Ephesians 6:16) – not some circumstances, not just difficult circumstances, but *all* circumstances, because the devil is sly and cunning, and his flaming darts can come from unexpected places. God has provided us with the ultimate protection for every spiritual battle, but it is absolutely useless if we don't put it on:

> Fight the good fight of the faith. Take hold of the eternal life to which you were called and about which you made the good confession in the presence of many witnesses.
> (1 Timothy 6:12)

Jesus is 'the author and finisher of our faith' (Hebrews 12:2, KJV), the Alpha and Omega of all things. He was there from the moment we stepped onto this narrow path, and He will be there until the day we make it home; then forevermore. He fought the ultimate battle and won, so during those times when we feel like giving up, we shift our focus and 'Consider him who endured from sinners such hostility against himself, so that you may not grow weary or faint-hearted' (Hebrews 12:3). Jesus has been there before us and He knows all that we are facing. When we put our full trust in Him, He will give us the strength we need to overcome the enemy. The enemy may start the fight, but the battle belongs to the Lord. For this reason, we can take hold of the eternal life to which we were called, remembering that what we face now is only temporary. One day the fight will end, and how great it will be to be able to say, 'I have fought the good fight, I have finished the race, I have kept the faith' (2 Timothy 4:7).

Keeping the faith

Not one of us can keep the faith through our own strength alone. Even with all the will and determination in the world, this earthly body and mind is just too weak and damaged by sin. The disciples were with Jesus day after day, month after month, and yet they too experienced feelings of being inadequately equipped, which caused them to ask the Lord, 'Increase our faith!' (Luke 17:5). The psalmist, David, tells us, 'The steps of a man are established by the LORD, when he delights in his way' (Psalm 37:23). This narrow path is *His way* and our steps are made sure when His teachings become our anchor points.

We keep the faith by keeping true to God's Word, by carrying it in our heart and committing to it with all of our soul. As the Lord said to Moses concerning the kings of Israel:

> When he sits on the throne of his kingdom, he shall write for himself in a book a copy of this law, approved by the Levitical priests. And it shall be with him, and he shall read in it all the days of his life, that he may learn to fear the LORD his God by keeping all the words of this law and these statutes, and doing them.
> (Deuteronomy 17:18-19)

Each king of Israel was required to write out a copy of God's law, keep it to hand at all times and commit himself to being faithful to it in all that he would do. God's Word would provide the king with knowledge and wisdom for every challenge that he would face. It would keep his heart pure, for 'the words of the LORD are pure' (Psalm 12:6), and it would keep his path sure, for it would be 'a lamp to [his] feet and a light [for his] path' (Psalm 119:105).

To keep the faith, God's Word needs to infuse every part of our being and flow through us as the lifeblood that it truly is. As the Lord commanded Joshua, saying, 'This Book of the Law shall not depart from your mouth, but you shall meditate on it day and night' (Joshua 1:8), so He commands us. We need to carry the words that are contained in God's precious book with us at all times – in our hearts and in our minds, 'For the word of God is living and active, sharper than any two-edged sword, piercing to the division of soul and of spirit' (Hebrews 4:12).

This is why we carry it and why the kings of old were to carry it. This holy sword pierces through the flesh (the sin-shell), separating that which is sinful from that which is holy. It cuts through the lies of the devil and reveals the truth of God. It convicts us when we go our own way, and directs us back to the right path:

> What does the LORD your God require of you, but to fear the LORD your God, to walk in all his ways, to love him, to serve the LORD your God with all your heart and with all your soul.
> (Deuteronomy 10:12)

You have probably heard the expression of putting your heart and soul into something, meaning all of your determination, all of your effort, all of your energy. This is the measure of commitment God made towards us when He said, 'Behold, I am with you and will keep you wherever you go ... For I will not leave you until I have done what I have promised you' (Genesis 28:15). This promise ultimately led to His beloved Son, Jesus, laying down His life for us. In view of God's steadfast love and faithful commitment to us, should we not also continually bring the same attitude of commitment to Him as we strive to follow the teachings of Jesus and to serve the Lord our God?

Sometimes we make the mistake of thinking that parts of God's Word do not apply to us personally because they were spoken to a specific individual or group of people. For example, although the words of the Lord quoted from Genesis 28:15 are part of Jacob's unfolding story, they are not there for the purpose of telling us *about* Jacob; their purpose is to tell us about God. Does God favour any one of His children above another? Is there one of us who is more deserving than anyone else? Do we not all fall short of God's standards? There is no favouritism in God's kingdom. He offers His mercy and grace equally to all, and His promises are given equally to all who give their lives to follow Him, for 'God is faithful, by whom you were called into the fellowship of his Son, Jesus Christ our Lord' (1 Corinthians 1:9).

The God of Jacob is our God and He does not intend for any of His children to walk this path alone. He will keep us always and He will never leave our side until that day when we stand victorious, side by side with every brother and sister in Christ – heirs of the King – united as one in eternal adoration and worship:

> Hallelujah!
> For the Lord our God
> the Almighty reigns.
> Let us rejoice and exult
> and give him the glory.
> (Revelation 19:6-7)

Reflections

Questions

- Think about what it means to put on the full armour of God. How does each piece protect us from the attack of the enemy?

- From reading this book, do you know something about God, Jesus and the Holy Spirit that you didn't know before? What is that, and how has it impacted you?

- What have you learned about who you are as a child of God that you didn't appreciate before? How will this affect your life from now on?

Practical application

Write down one thing from each chapter in the book that will help you to walk this narrow path from this point on. Meditate on these things, and pray on them.

Prayer

Lord Jesus, thank You for coming down to this earth and for paving the way that would lead me back to God. Thank You for dying for me. Thank You for my salvation. Help me to live by the lessons that You have taught as I let the truth of Your Word fill my heart and mind. Strengthen me day by day, Lord; guard my steps and help me to grow a deep-rooted faith in You. Amen.

Make me to know your ways, O LORD;
teach me your paths.
Lead me in your truth and teach me,
for you are the God of my salvation;
for you I wait all the day long.

(Psalm 25:4-5)

Note from the author

What a journey this has been! I never imagined that devotionals I had written at the start of 2021 ('Lessons from the Teacher') would be the basis from which this book would grow. I had felt God nudging me forward and yet I let self-doubt hold me back – for a little while at least. At the beginning of 2023, I lifted the barriers and trusted this promise: 'I will instruct you and teach you in the way you should go; I will counsel you with my eye upon you' (Psalm 32:8). I allowed God to lead me by His Spirit on this amazing writing journey, knowing that He was with me every step of the way. I feel incredibly blessed to have been given this opportunity; it has been quite the adventure and it's not over yet!

To my husband, Neil, who graciously walked this path with me as I locked myself away for days and weeks at a time: thank you so much for all the lunches and dinners that were waiting for me, and the endless cups of coffee that appeared right on time. Thank you for allowing me to grumble at you as you corrected my grammar and pointed out my use of colloquialisms. Thank you for reading and rereading, every time I made a change – in everything, you have helped me to make this book better. The freedom I have to spend my days writing are all down to you, and for that I cannot thank you enough.

To Phil Howe, for reading and critiquing the manuscript, then writing the foreword – thank you. From the first moment I mentioned this book you were completely on board, and I am so grateful for your encouragement and support through every leg of the journey.

To Roger Abrol, a spiritual mentor for more than twenty years and a dear friend for more than forty – thank you for reading the first draft and for your detailed critique (I wasn't expecting anything less). You were instrumental in my growth as a Christian, and through this project you have helped me grow as a writer.

To Janet Broad and Roberta Courtney – as I pushed to get the initial edit completed and you realised that I was slightly overwhelmed and my brain was turning to mush, you said, 'Can we help?' You didn't have to ask twice, and fifteen minutes later you both had copies of the manuscript. I am incredibly grateful for all your comments and suggestions regarding the questions that follow each chapter, as well as the practical applications. Your help allowed me to breathe – thank you – that meant a lot.

I was apprehensive about asking for endorsements and I prayed that the Lord would lead me to the right people. My sincere thanks go to Rick, Michael, Trevor and Dave for, first of all, taking time out of their busy schedules to read the manuscript and, second, for their words that encourage others to read this book for themselves.

I have had a lot of support and encouragement over the last four years from those who read the devotionals that I send out each week. I am especially grateful for all the prayer that was offered up in response to my request, that the right publisher would be found. Thank you for praying for me and for this book; it is very much appreciated.

In answer to those prayers, God led me to Nicki Copeland and the team at Instant Apostle, a truly godly Christian publisher. I want to thank them for seeing the potential in that first submitted draft and for joining with me in this, somewhat surreal, adventure. Your advice and attention to detail has been invaluable, and your genuine care has made this process an absolute joy.

My ultimate thanks I lift up to God for leading me on this amazing journey and for challenging me with every chapter that was written. Through it all, He led me into a deeper relationship with Him – Father, Son and Spirit. I now hand this book back to Him and pray that it will be used for His glory and that all who read it will be encouraged to develop their own deep relationship with God.